A Contemporary
Classroom Classic!

Educating Congregations

The Future of Christian Education

Charles R. Foster

Abingdon Press
Nashville

EDUCATING CONGREGATIONS
The Future of Christian Education
Copyright © 1994 by Abingdon Press
Preface Copyright © 2006

This book is printed on acid-free paper.

Library of Congress Cataloging-in-Publication Data

Foster, Charles R., 1937-
    Educating congregations: the future of Christian education /
Charles R. Foster.
        p.   cm
    ISBN 0-687-00245-1 (alk. paper)
    1. Christian education. 2. Christianity—Forecasting. 3. Church
work.   I. Title.
VVI464.F65   1994
268—dc20
ISBN-13: 978-0-687-00245-0

07 08 09 10 11—20 19 18 17 16
MANUFACTURED IN THE UNITED STATES OF AMERICA

To
LEE R. and *NAOMI E. FOSTER,*

whose visions for teaching and learning
first filled my imagination
with the possibilities in
church education for
building communities of faith
engaged in quests
for meaning and hope
relevant to the times in which we live.

Contents

Preface

I originally wrote Educating Congregations because it was my perception that congregations needed to be reminded that a lack of commitment to education was threatening the future of their mission as the body of Christ in the world. The current revival of religiosity in the United States would suggest that my perception might be wrong. Mega-churches are attracting multitudes, religiously inspired movements are shaping public opinion and policy, and missional congregations are engaging in life-changing ministries. This religious activism is significant, but it also hides an amazing lack of attention to tasks that ensure the future relevance and vitality of their ministries.

I did discover congregations here and there that do take seriously the task of cultivating the future of their mission through their education. Informed by their experience, I propose in *Educating Congregations* ways to think more effectively about the practices for cultivating their future participation in the formative and transformative events of Christian tradition.

I now realize I had anticipated the discussion of Christian practices by Dorothy Bass, et al., in *Practicing Our Faith* (1997) and by Craig Dykstra in *Growing in the Life of Faith* (1999). I drew extensively on the language of practice in writing the book but without their consciousness of its social and theological function or educational structure. Their insights clarify and deepen my assumptions about the role of a community's practices in cultivating its future. Those assumptions include, but are not limited to the following:

• As congregations engage their members in practices that give form and content to their participation in the formative and transformative events of Christian tradition and mission

7

they both transmit and cultivate a distinctive "way-of-life"—a Christian way-of-being in the world.

• Those who participate in formative and transformative practices integral to the events of Christian tradition and mission learn or take up that "way-of-life" as apprentice disciples by rehearsing them over and again in their congregational particularity—e.g., as Methodists, Catholics, or Baptists. As they identify with the intent of those practices they increasingly take on the identity, dispositions, habits, and ways of thinking associated with that congregation's participation in and engagement with those events.

• Participants in the practices of the events of Christian tradition and mission develop expertise in this "way-of-life" as they live into expectations in those events for how they might live, think, and act. These expectations establish standards for critiquing the knowledge and skill they bring to their engagement in those events, for entering into dialogue with the knowledge, dispositions, and habits—or ways-of-life—of other communities, and for the renewal and transformation of personal faith and congregational life.

For busy pastors, religious educators, and lay leaders and teachers the challenge of developing a vibrant and faithful education in a congregation may seem daunting. And yet, the tasks remain urgent. In the following chapters, I explore three of these tasks: 1) building up congregations as communities of faith to be the body of Christ in this fragmented world; 2) developing the ability to identify and articulate the relevance of the gospel in an age inundated with information and confused by new knowledge; and 3) nurturing hope among peoples overwhelmed by wars, natural disasters, social, economic, and health crises. In *Educating Congregations*, I propose that instead of some new educational program, we take seriously learning how to participate in the formative and transformative events of the Christian tradition and witness. In the practices devoted to that effort I see a future for Christian education.

Charles R. Foster, 2006

Acknowledgments

IN ONE FORM OR ANOTHER I have been working on the themes in this book for most of the thirty years since my graduation from Union Theological Seminary in New York in 1963. Declining enrollments in church education, intensifying curricular battles over what should be taught and how, diminishing standards for an ever smaller pool of well-trained teachers, and losing battles over increasingly limited financial resources for the support of Christian education in denominational bureaucracies and seminary programs repeatedly awakened me to a growing dilemma for the future of the church.

At the same time the visionary thinking of teachers and colleagues continued to provide inspiration to those of us struggling to find a way to speak to the sociological, economic, and institutional changes affecting the quality of teaching and learning in the church. As I complete this manuscript I thank my teachers: C. Ellis Nelson, Robert W. Lynn, Lawrence Cremin, Sara Little; mentors and colleagues in local church education: Eugene E. Laubach, Ethel Johnson, Norma Barsness, Tom Steen, and the members of "The Twenty"; colleagues who persist in their quest for a more adequate vision of church education: Robert L. Browning, Everett Tilson, Jack Seymour, Robert O'Gorman, John and Ad Carr, James Fowler, and Don Richter; and participants in several conferences and lectures who listened and gave me feedback on various parts of the chapters that follow: the Jones Lectures at Austin Presbyterian Theological Seminary, the Conference on Ministries with Children sponsored by the United Methodist Pacific Southwest Annual Conference, the Iliff Theological Seminary Ministers Week,

9

the Candler Christian Education Conference. I am also indebted to the gracious people of the First United Methodist Church in Arlington, Texas, Overton Park United Methodist Church in Fort Worth, and Hope United Methodist Church in San Diego who took up the task of revisioning the education of their congregations; and to those who read and critiqued the manuscript: Jack Seymour, Bob O'Gorman, Duane Ewers, Ted Brelsford, John Pitney, and Martha Forrest. Their encouragement and suggestions have significantly shaped this work.

Introduction

THE EDUCATIONAL CHALLENGE BEFORE the churches of North America is an urgent one. Educational structures originally developed to help establish and extend Christian societies in the vast open spaces and new cities of the United States and Canada are increasingly irrelevant to the efforts of contemporary churches to maintain a Christian vision for a pluralistic and technological global village. Two parables illumine this challenge for the churches. In the first, a chief of the Digger Indians of California attempts to convey his understanding of the situation of his people to the anthropologist Ruth Benedict. He uses a graphic image.

> In the beginning God gave to every people a cup, a cup of clay, and from this cup they drank their life. They all dipped in the water, but their cups were different. Our cup is broken now. It has passed away.[1]

European diseases had decimated the tribal population. Immigrants had shoved them from their tribal homelands. The chief could no longer envision a future for his people. The cup sustaining their life had shattered.

The cup that holds the future of any nation, any community, any congregation is always fragile. Conflicts between religious or ethnic groups leading to war, famine and disease, natural disasters, and social or economic calamities have always threatened the future of human communities. But the most serious threat to any community's future occurs when its education can no longer maintain its heritage into the present or renew its identity or vocation for its changing circumstances. The signs pointing to the diminishing effectiveness of the

11

church's education are everywhere. Declining enrollments in church education classrooms, diminishing
influence of congregations on the moral tone of their
neighborhoods, persisting racism, sexism, and classism in
our churches and their larger communities, increasing
evidence of biblical illiteracy and theological naïveté,
increasing reliance on marketing strategies to attract and
hold new members, and an overwhelming lack of attention to our stewardship of the earth reveal deep flaws, if
not broken educational structures for the maintenance
and renewal of church identity and mission.

A second parable is more hopeful. It also has to do
with a shattered pot. In this instance God tells the
prophet Jeremiah to visit a potter. Jeremiah arrives at the
designated shop to discover him at work shaping a pot. It
spoils in his hand. So "he reworked it into another vessel,
as seemed good to him" (Jer. 18:4b). Jeremiah discerned
in the destruction and refashioning of the pot a sign of
hope for the Israelites. The clay was not useless; it could
be refashioned. An apostate nation could once again
become faithful. A fickle people could once again contribute effectively to the mission of God. I hope this is
the situation in which we find ourselves. The vessel giving shape to church education is flawed. It needs to be
refashioned.[2] Perhaps if we heed the signs that reveal
flaws in church education, we have time to envision a
new structure for nurturing our common lives as Christians.

We have been warned of the seriousness of our situation before. Over thirty years ago James Smart warned us
that the "strange silence of the Bible in our churches"
could be traced to problems in our education. More
than fifteen years ago John Westerhoff warned us that
our educational efforts did not necessarily lead children
to Christian faith. More recently John Hull, a religious
educator in England, pointedly wondered why Christian

adults can't learn. A study of effective Christian education in six mainline denominations by the Search Institute in Minneapolis confirms their fears. Contemporary
church education falters in its efforts to build up faith
communities capable of incarnating Christ's ministries of
love and justice appropriate to God's mission at the junc-
ture of the twentieth and twenty-first centuries.[3]

This brings me to my thesis. It is a simple one. The
congregation is the context, and its mission—to praise
God and serve neighbors—the impetus for Christian religious education. The purpose of church education flows
out of these two statements. It is to "build up" or construct communities of faith to praise God and serve
neighbors for the sake of the "emancipatory transformation of the world," which New Testament writers envisioned as the Kingdom of God.[4] In this corporate educational effort the nurture of the faith and the practice of
the witness of community members occur.

My thesis is not original. It reflects the insights of Jewish exiles in Babylon and first-century Christians living
expectantly into a new age. More recently it stands in the
religious education tradition of C. Ellis Nelson's conviction that congregations embody the traditions of Christian faith and through their corporate lives communicate
the meanings of faith to the next generation by the way
they worship and live together. It shares Westerhoff's
conviction that the meanings of faith are nurtured in the
interplay of congregational processes of formation and
education. It holds with Jack Seymour, Margaret Ann
Crain, and Joseph V. Crockett that the meanings arising
from faith learning occur at the intersection of the
human quest for identity and vocation. These and other
scholars have significantly shaped my thinking. What I
hope to offer in this book is creative and practical appli-
cation of my own and others' insights so that congregations can grow in faith.

I strongly support a corporate view of education, a process the apostle Paul called "building up" the body of Christ. Only in communities seeking to *incarnate* Christ's presence can our personal quests for Christian faith, identity, and vocation be nurtured. Education is a historical process, gathering up, renewing, and transforming the visions for community originating in the wider fellowship of the apostles of Jesus. Church education occurs consequently, whenever and wherever congregations seek to transmit, interpret, and create attitudes, knowledge, skills, habits, sensibilities or perspectives integral to the transformative ministries of God in and through the worship and mission of the church. Therefore, when describing the congregation or parish as the context and impetus for a new vision for the education of Christian communities, our attention is directed to the reconfiguration of the congregation's life as we know it. This transformation will not be easy. It will require commitment and courage.

I wrote this book to assist pastors, Christian educators and lay leaders in congregations and parishes where people want to explore new, more responsive educational models. The text has been written to be read either by an individual or in group settings. Exercises and discussion questions interrupt the text to facilitate this process.

Chapter 1 directs readers to explore flaws in the structures and procedures that influence and guide their congregation's educational ministries.

Chapter 2 proposes an alternative image to the "school" for organizing church education.

Chapters 3, 4, and 5 focus on three educational tasks that flow out of a congregation's efforts to build up a community of faith dedicated to a vocation of worship and mission. These tasks focus on building community in chapter 3 and making meaning in chapter 4.

Chapter 5 explores the task of embodying hope as the impetus to congregational and personal vocation.

The book concludes with a guide congregational leaders may use to implement insights from this study to strengthen their local church educational ministries. The guide may be photocopied to facilitate the work of the committee or task force that takes up this responsibility. In that effort, if my readers discover clues to the future of an education in their own congregation that culminates in a more adequate praise of God and service of neighbor, my purposes for writing this book will have been realized.

EXERCISE IN CONGREGATIONAL ANALYSIS

Before reading chapter 1, list all the times and places where people in your congregation are engaged in Christian education. These include

- classes
- study groups
- informational bulletin boards
- choir rehearsals
- special programs designed to teach something

Be specific. Examples are: all Sunday school classes, worship readiness sessions for children, new member orientation, and sermons that interpret scripture.

When the list is complete, review it to identify strengths and problems you see in your congregation's education.

1.

Flaws in the Church Education Vessel

A STORY FOR OUR TIME

Once upon a time a congregation took seriously its educational responsibilities.[1] Its members knew the stories of the Bible and the saints in the church's history. Their imaginations were enlivened by the poetry of the psalms and the hymns of worship. They knew the prayers, creeds, and many of the hymns by memory. They engaged in acts of compassion and sought justice for the hungry, homeless, dispossessed, alienated, and marginalized.

This congregation taught its children from a very young age. Adults told them stories of God's faithfulness over and over again. They taught children hymns of praise and thanksgiving until they were so familiar the children often sang them in their play. They involved children in the practice of praying in the manner of Jesus. They visited sacred places together and engaged in acts of service among people hurting and hungering for the bounty of God's love and benefice. They explored the scriptures and traditions of faith together for clues to moral decision making and faithful living.

After these children had grown, a crisis fell on this congregation and its community. The form of the crisis makes little difference to the outcome of this story. It could have been caused by an act of nature: a tornado, flood, drought, or earthquake. It could have been caused by an economic depression or war that stretched loyalties and moral commitments. It could have been precipitated by an internal conflict among church members over church teachings, practices, or programs.

In the midst of the crisis, the members of this congregation remembered the sacred places and took their children to visit them. They probed the ancient stories for clues to the crisis. They sang and prayed through their anxieties, frustrations, and confusion. They listened and watched for signs to lead them out of the crisis. They shared their money, food, clothing, and shelter with victims of the crisis.

They survived. Although weary and filled with grief over those who had been hurt and lost during the experience, they continued to praise God, serve their neighbors, and teach their children by precept and example.

Years later another crisis hit the congregation. Again the nature of the crisis is not important, but this time its members were not as prepared for its severity. When they had been children, their teachers had read to them stories from scripture. They sang several hymns often enough to recognize them when they came upon them in the hymnal. They had been introduced to the primary doctrines of the church's heritage during confirmation. The pastor and one or two wise lay leaders answered their faith and moral questions when asked. The congregation's sacred places continued to provide comfort and an occasional moment of inspiration. Parents made sure their children participated in religious education classes whenever they were in town, took them to special Christmas and Easter worship events, and sent them to educational programs during summer vacations. But for many people in the congregation the connections between the experience in church and the issues, decisions, and circumstances of their lives did not seem very obvious.

When this second crisis enveloped the congregation,

some people gathered to pray and to listen to the advice of the pastor. A core of congregational leaders explored biblical and church traditions with the pastor for clues to living faithfully through the crisis. Some adults remembered a few hymns and prayers from their childhood. A few children were reminded of the longtime relationship their families had had with the church. They eventually survived the crisis—a little weary and worn from the experience, but praising God for blessings they discovered in their time of trial.

And so the congregation continued to meet on that street corner for many more years. Changes in the church corresponded to changes in the community. Many people who had grown up in the congregation moved away. New people who did not know the congregation's history joined its fellowship. The church competed for people's time with work, leisure, and school schedules. Parents did not know the stories, hymns, and prayers well enough to teach them to their children. They no longer knew the location of the places that had been sacred to their ancestors, although a few of the older members knew they were listed in an ancient directory stored in the church library. The congregation had difficulty finding teachers, and few adults knew the names of the children who passed them in the halls or sat near them during worship. Only a few older members of the congregation had any real familiarity with the doctrines, traditions, and rituals that had enlivened the congregation's past. To most the words seemed archaic and strange—even offensive.

Although the congregation continued to sponsor religious education classes, many children did not know the words to the Lord's Prayer. Many stumbled over the strange language of the creed. Few had a sense of the sweep of the story of God's love for Israel. The stories of Jesus seemed quaint. The scriptures were rarely used by their parents to explore the ethical issues confronting them. The pastor and lay leaders spent most of their time planning programs, managing church finances, listening to people's problems, and maintaining the church building. Every once in awhile the pastor would lead some people to one of the sacred places to tell a story that had enlivened the imaginations of their great-grandparents and people would glimpse something of the power of the faith that had built that place.

A crisis again fell upon this congregation. Many were so busy they did not even notice. Some older members gathered to pray for the congregation. The administration committee appointed a task force to address the situation, but its members did not know what to do, so they hired a consultant to guide them. The choir director taught the congregation a few choruses to increase a sense of participation in worship. The pastor preached a series of sermons on the crisis. Children joined the pastor on the chancel steps for a special "sermon" each Sunday during the worship service. The education committee ordered a new curriculum.

Did the congregation survive? We do not know yet, because that is the situation in which most congregations now find themselves. In a recent study of Christian education in six major denominations, the Search Institute discovered a vast difference in the maturity of faith between those over sixty and those under.[2] This study points to a strange situation. For at least the past fifty years, the identification of people in the church with the sources and meanings of Christian faith and tradition has decreased with each succeeding generation.

Several years ago in his popular book *Will Our Children Have Faith?* John Westerhoff warned the churches of this impending crisis. He wrote: "No longer can we assume that the educational understandings that have informed us, or the theological foundations that have undergirded our efforts, are adequate for the future."[3] His words caught our attention. We flocked to workshops and conferences to hear him. Seminary professors assigned the book to future pastors and Christian educators. But I discerned little attention to his question. I wondered why. Two possibilities occur to me.

Perhaps Westerhoff asked the wrong question. James Fowler, through his study of faith development and moral development, has helped us recognize that all persons have faith. To have faith is simply part of being human. We know our children will have faith. Increasingly, however, we have no idea what faith they will have. The increase of options for the faith commitment of our children has been a common part of the religious landscape since the late 1960s. Congregations, however, continue to act as if their children will automatically take on the identity and mission of the church as adults.

We may now discern a second reason people in the church may not have taken Westerhoff's question seriously. Churches have not acknowledged the diminishing capacity—even the brokenness—of their education. These churches are no longer capable of building up communities of faith adequate to the contemporary challenge of praising God and serving neighbor for the sake of the emancipatory transformation of the world.

EXERCISE IN CONGREGATIONAL ANALYSIS

Do you see signs of diminishing effectiveness in your congregation's education over the past twenty to thirty years? If so, what are they? How serious are they?

Is your congregation in the first, second, or third phase of the story or is it at some other point? Give examples to back up your conclusions. You may want to review attendance statistics for various educational programs and activities over the past five to ten years to document some of your hunches.

Keep a record of your answers to review when you read "A Guide to Revisioning Local Church Education."

LOCATING THE FLAWS
IN CHURCH EDUCATION

If we are to create a new vision for church education relevant to our present circumstances, we must be specific about the flaws in the structures and strategies of our current educational practice. As I have struggled over the years to understand changes taking place in church education, clues to five flaws in its goals and structures have become increasingly clear. They include: (1) the loss of communal memory in congregational life; (2) the irrelevance of our teaching about the Bible for contemporary life; (3) the subversion of educational goals; (4) the cultural captivity of church education; and (5) the collapse of the church's educational strategy. Let us take a brief look at these clues to deep and pervasive flaws in church education.

1. The Loss of Corporate Memory. Norma and Gene Johnson volunteered to teach a group of junior high youth using denominational curriculum resources.[4] The unit introduced the life and work of Paul to the young people. They began the first session of the series with several questions to discover what the young people remembered from previous encounters with Paul in their church experience. Two members of the group thought Paul had something to do with the New Testament. The rest could not recall having heard his name, anything about him, his ministry, or his writings.

Norma and Gene knew the young people had studied Paul's writings at other times in their Christian religious education experience. They knew many had heard sermons based on texts written by Paul. "Why can't they remember?" Norma asked. "If they cannot recall the great stories of faith, how will they know who they are?"

Gene wondered. Their complaint echoes an observation by E. D. Hirsch, Jr. An increasing proportion of the young people in the United States do not possess enough information to participate effectively in the "complex cooperative activities" of community life. He called this problem "cultural illiteracy"—a euphemism for the ignorance that enslaves people to the tyranny of their own experience. "Only by accumulating shared symbols, and the shared information that the symbols represent," Hirsch reminds us, "can we learn to communicate effectively with one another in our national community."[5] My concern goes a little deeper. Only by repeated and increasingly conscious participation in the shared events evoking our community's identity and vocation do we begin to discover in that community's memory resources for envisioning and constructing a future filled with meaning and hope. For Christians that future encompasses visions of shalom with God, neighbor, and the earth originating in the responses of our faith ancestors to the creative and providential acts of God.

Robert Wuthnow, the Director of the Center for the Study of American Religion at Princeton University, has explored the consequences of Norma and Gene's discovery in a comparison of two Gallup polls. In a poll taken in 1955, only 4 percent (or one person in twenty-five) left the faith traditions of their childhood. Some thirty years later, one out of every three persons had left the communal traditions of their childhood faith. This includes a significant proportion of youth and young adults who leave the church and will probably never return to any religious community.

These choices are now being made by children in fourth, fifth, and sixth grades. The historic rite of passage in North America in which the young leave the church of their parents for a time to decide whether or not they will continue to belong to it as adults has taken on new implications. "Most of us," according to Robert Bellah and his colleagues, "imagine" for ourselves, "an autonomous self existing independently, entirely outside any tradition and community." That expectation of autonomy denies any value in identifying with the future possibilities of ancestral traditions and experience. It rejects the importance of nurturing a communal memory. The Search Institute describes this problem as a diminishing loyalty to our faith communities. It is deeper. It is the loss of our connectedness across the ages—a loss that diminishes the intensity of our sense of identification with the followers of Jesus in the past and for the future.[6]

2. The Irrelevance of Our Teaching from the Bible. A second clue to the flaws in the church's education became clear to me during one of several conversations with Jack Forester. Jack is now in his early eighties. He has taught an adult Bible class in his small congregation for many of the past forty years. He prepares diligently for each session, working through the curriculum resources provided by his denomination and through a set of commentaries and other Bible study helps he has collected. Almost every time I meet Jack he expresses frustration with the curriculum resources. "They never answer my questions," he complains. "What would you like to know?" I ask. He typically answers my question with two requests. He would like more information about the influence of the historical situation surrounding specific scripture passages and narratives on their meaning for people at the time of their composition. And he would like more guidance on ways to discover the relevance of those ancient words for the very different circumstances in which he now lives. "The Bible is an ancient book. It makes little sense if we cannot interpret its message for our own situation," he concludes.

For Jack the problem in the church's education is the danger that without interpretation, biblical and theological resources written in the past have little relevance to the faith questions of people today. I would suggest another. When church education does not introduce lay leaders like Jack Forester to methods of theological reflection on biblical and theological texts, they are confined to their own opinions and interpretations. The effects are seen in laity who, like Jack, sense there must be more to biblical faith than they experience, and among others, who cannot see anything in the Bible relevant to their lives.

I experienced this latter problem directly in a youth ministry class I taught for seminary students. Each student in the class interviewed a teenager actively involved in a congregation. These interviews included a series of questions on how the youth understood the Golden Rule. Over the years a persistent theme emerged from these conversations. Many youth could not see its usefulness as a principle for their conduct. One eighteen-year-old high school senior summed up their feelings: "It is hard to do. People just don't understand a person" who tries to follow the Golden Rule. It could help people "learn to respect each other more" but "I don't see this happening."[7] For many young and older people the Bible has become irrelevant to their quest for meaning and purpose.

The problem, however, is not the irrelevance of the Bible. It is the irrelevance of the ways we teach from the Bible. This irrelevance in our teaching is often ironic. The theological naïveté in the approach of many church folk to the Bible contrasts with their sophisticated and complex conversations about scientific, social, political, economic, agricultural, and interpersonal matters. Sources of that naïveté are deeply rooted in the educational practices of our churches. In a passionate essay,

Edward Farley, a contemporary theologian concerned about the education of the whole church, traces the problem to the "almost uncrossable gulf between theological [clergy] and church [lay] education." Why, he wonders, has the church essentially settled for "the premodern pattern of educated clergy and uneducated laity?"[8] An obvious answer may point to a relatively unconscious conspiracy. Theologically trained clergy, religious educators, and curriculum policy decision makers have withheld from laity the methods and skills to interpret the scriptures and to engage in theological reflection capable of opening up their deepest questions and illumining their most hidden doubts.

Jack Forester experienced that conspiracy more than once. One of his pastors suggested he keep his questions about the Bible to himself. One asked him to stop teaching the class he had helped teach for more than twenty years because the pastor felt his teaching might disturb the faith of some of its members. A student of mine experienced another form of this conspiracy when his pastor criticized his attempts to introduce adults in a Bible class to some basic methods of interpretation: "You don't want people to start thinking do you?" he was asked. Users of most church education curriculum resources unknowingly experience this conspiracy because publishers, seeking to avoid controversies that might limit sales, limit reader engagement with biblical texts to relatively uncontroversial interpretations and approaches to theological reflection. In the sixteenth century powerful church leaders sought to keep the words of scripture from laity. Today laity have the words but lack the methods of biblical interpretation and theological reflection possessed by scholars and clergy to discover how to read ancient texts from the standpoint of their lives at the edge of the twenty-first century.

3. The Subversion of Christian Educational Goals. Historically, the goals of Christian religious education have emphasized, in John Wesley's words, salvation and sanctification. The former focused on our relationship with God and the latter on the quality and character of our living, especially in relation to our neighbor. Concepts like conversion and nurture, catechesis and faith development, personal and social transformation illumine their strategic implications. Despite the familiarity of these ideas in church conversations about educating for faith, I am increasingly convinced that most North American churches—conservative or liberal, orthodox or nontraditional—actually sponsor an education more dependent on popular understandings of psychology, therapy, and marketing.

Preference for psychological, therapeutic, and marketing rather than theological sources for churches thinking about their education may be seen most clearly in the shift of religious education goals from salvation and sanctification to the "needs" of learners. "Needs" are defined primarily in psychological categories, sometimes disguised by religious language. Since they are internal and subjective they often collapse into what individual learners want. Since learning is defined as meeting needs, teaching is directed to satisfying student needs and wants. From this perspective church education becomes the organizational mechanism for meeting the needs of people. Publicity campaigns then urge people in the church and community to participate in classes and other educational activities designed to meet those needs.

This commitment to the learning of individuals in our churches as the basis for religious change reached its peak in the emphasis given by religious educators to "learning by objective" during the 1970s. For some churches (mostly with a conservative theology) this meant that if teachers could develop objectives precise enough to fit specific learner needs, then they believed they could precipitate a conversion of faith among their students. For other churches (mostly with a liberal theology) this meant that if teachers could create an educational environment reflecting the values and spirit of Christian community in its most desirable form, students would take on in a natural way, the thinking and life-style of the community.

Church school teachers, Christian educators, and pastors, however, constantly encounter the practical limits of these approaches to training Christians. Sporadic attendance undercuts the consistency required to support the voluntary learning of individuals. Few teachers, whether volunteer or professional—possess the skill to respond to critical moments of individual student learning, if they discern them, or the time to work with the variety of student questions and struggles they encounter. Curriculum resources cannot be written to respond to the range of personal or group concerns or expectations. The inability of congregations to sustain an educational ministry for the individual learning of children, youth, or adults has culminated in the subversion of most church education into learning activities designed to enrich student religious experience rather than to build up transformed and transformative communities of faith.

Enrichment education seeks to create a positive experience for students—from having a good time in a hospitable place for young children to initiating a lively discussion among youth or adults. In this regard it moves closer to the dynamics of entertainment than to the transformation of life. Its concern is to promote a momentary sense of well-being or self-esteem in the student. Since the focus of a teacher's attention is on a given session rather than to the development of a teaching relationship over time, there is little concern about continuity or about a developing competency in the knowledge and habits of faith. Teachers can rotate in and out of a classroom to fit their personal schedules. Topics and themes are interchangeable. Traditional teachings—especially those that address our human proclivity to sin and disobedience—are often trivialized or recast to reflect the value system of the larger community.

The shift to enrichment education is most evident, however, in the tendency among many church leaders to reduce congregational education to *programs* for teaching and learning. In such congregations the professional Christian educator often becomes the program director or coordinator of parish life. Apparently early advocates of the shift of language to program never pondered the meaning of the term they were adopting. A program is a list of events to be performed, a plan of activities to be completed. It emphasizes entertainment rather than learning, consumption rather than transformation. It tends to embody the values and structures of the shopping mall. People are offered a wide range of choices.

Larger and more affluent congregations can make more choices available. Smaller and less affluent congregations struggle with limited leadership and resources to offer a single program for everyone. In both large and small congregations people participate on their own terms. They browse among the options offered, and if something catches their attention, they commit themselves to it for a time. Program options emphasize personal choice, often without criteria to assess the relative value of the options offered (so any book, method, topic, or issue is acceptable as long as some people are interested in it and it does not offend the beliefs and sensitivities of the majority). Differences of taste and opinion are tolerated, but the differences in what people bring to the church education marketplace (gender, cultural, socioeconomic, and educational experience) are not valued as gifts to any kind of common life.[9] Large congregations expend their energies in futile attempts to offer something for everyone, often in a way that reduces the role of Christian educators and pastors to office managers and program gofers. Small congregations become immobilized by the intensity of their awareness of the lack of sufficient resources.

To view education as a "program" bankrupts a congregation's efforts to initiate "people into the ways of thinking and behaving characteristic" of the heritage of the church and to "recreate itself" to extend the life and mission of the church into the future.[10] Individual persons may have a good experience. Learning does take place—sometimes in significant ways. But an identity and mission for the congregation's future is never identified. Programmatic enrichment education actually creates the conditions to intensify a sense of isolation rather than community because the bonds are internal and personal rather than external. They emphasize personal needs and/or interests. They focus on instant rather than sustained intimacy. From this perspective the slightest shift in temperament, perspective, or commitment shatters the fragile consensus of mutuality that exists among persons in a learning group. It locates the authority for our decisions in ourselves rather than in any kind of relationship with a transcendent reality or in the historicity of our common life. From this perspective the encounters of the Hebrews, the early church, or the saints through the ages with God seem strange and archaic. The transformational character of the gospel is muted by the "psychological moss" of therapeutic teaching methodologies that effectively subvert the contribution of the church's education to the future vitality of the corporate Christian witness.[11]

4. The Cultural Captivity of Church Education. A clue to one of the most serious flaws in the church's education has been its proclivity to sanction the cultural status quo rather than to embrace the transformational message of the gospel for the emancipation of people from their spiritual, social, political, or economic bondage. In the history of the United States and Canada, the church's education has been used to alienate native peoples from their cultural heritage and to oppress enslaved and marginalized peoples. It has perpetuated patterns of cultural dominance among immigrants and sustained the dominance of patriarchal perspectives and practices in the organization of church education and in the content of church teaching.[12]

The story of the cultural captivity of the church's education is often painful. The residue of nineteenth century teachings about human relations persist to this day in the racism, sexism, ageism, classism, and other "isms" diminishing God's intentions for all people. A poem appearing in a Sunday school story paper for children in 1885 may illustrate the first half of my point. Accompanying the poem is a drawing of a small child with fair skin and blond hair and another small child with dark skin and black hair gathered into tight pigtails. The child with blond hair has a scrub brush in her hand.

> No, Becky, be quiet!
> I can't let you go;
> Your mamma has never
> Half washed you, I know.
> With nice soap and water
> And brush, I must try
> To make you as white and
> As clean as I
> So Becky don't cry.

> I feel very sorry
> When nice little girls
> Have mammas who don't like
> To unscrew their curls,
> Nor keep them washed nicely,
> As children should be;
> I'll give you a scrubbing,
> And then we shall see
> How white you will be![13]

The words offend us. We say we would never be guilty of such blatant racism. But the lack of gospel in this poem written for church children is only a less sophisticated version of the ethnocentricity I recently ran across in a description for a resource for a multicultural education for young children. This resource book is designed to help teachers nurture

> the cultural instincts of young learners by enhancing **each child's experience** (emphasis mine) in a sensitive, respectful way. Based on the pattern of learning for young children, activities originate with familiar ideas— bread, for instance—and lead children to explore less familiar ones such as tortillas, pita and matzo.[14]

A curriculum unit that begins with the assumption that its readers will primarily be familiar with bread, communicates a clear message to those who are more familiar with tortillas, pita, or matzo that they do not belong to the group using this curriculum resource. This kind of insensitivity to racial, ethnic, social class, and gender issues in particular, has contributed to many distortions in the church's education. When church education engages in the transmission of its heritage without critically examining the ways its cultural bias limits the gospel, it stifles the transformatory character of the message it seeks to proclaim. Words of grace, redemption, and love, consequently, all too often are then heard as words of pain, alienation, and suffering. In the changing dynamics of the relationships of male and female and of the many cultures in the human community, any church education that equates the gospel with the perspectives of a particular cultural, social, or economic standard is flawed.

5. *The Collapse of the Church's Educational Strategy.* So far we have been exploring sources for the flaws in church education to be found in the congregation. Now we turn to changes in the social and cultural systems outside the congregation that affect its ability to build the corporate faith of its members to praise God and serve neighbors. Clues to the changing systemic dynamics affecting church education are often heard in the complaints of church leaders about the lack of parental cooperation and support, the competition for time by schools and other community activities, the difficulty in recruiting volunteers willing to take the time to do a good job, and the lack of clergy involvement in the educational life of the congregation. Often these complaints arise from nostalgic comparisons with an earlier era when the Bible was regularly read (at least in some homes), parents assumed they should volunteer to teach, schools did not schedule activities on Sundays or on Wednesday nights, churches had a strong corps of people dedicated to a vocation of teaching, business and civic leaders gave leadership to church education as an expression of their civic duty, and families ordered much of their leisure time and social life around congregational or parish activities.

Times have changed. Changing family and work patterns radically limit congregational dependence on volunteers for church education leadership. The proliferation of school programs and community and leisure activities expand the options for the time and energy of children, youth, and adults. The media industries shape the organization of our days and influence the patterns of our relationships. Television has brought technologically sophisticated entertainment into our homes. Compact disks and tapes make it possible to be surrounded by music any place and time. Through computers we can communicate with people across the street and around the world without ever seeing them.

These profound changes in the systemic structures of the communities in which church education is located radically circumscribe its role in the community and its place in the lives of people. Little support exists in our communities for sustained church efforts to provide a Christian religious education. When congregations seek to educate religiously, in other words, they are, in most communities, the only place where Christian values and perspectives are fully affirmed and communicated.

Church education, however, faces a second structural problem. Although the specific stories among Protestant and Catholic parishes vary, during the past twenty years denominational structures to support the education of congregations have been radically curtailed. Just at that point in history when social and economic changes necessitated the intensification of denominational support for education in the congregation, staff have been cut, training programs reduced almost to nothing, standards diminished and/or discarded, and networks of persons concerned about the quality of the church's education dissipated.

Marketing, rather than religious education concerns, increasingly dominates the goals of curriculum design and production. Collaborative efforts among denominations focus more on survival than on shaping the future. Consequently, few congregations now have an adequate core of persons with the vision, training, and experience to sustain educational ministries capable of creating a faithful and viable future for congregational life. To fill this gap an increasing number of churches have hired people—many relatively untrained—to manage their educational ministries or programs in an effort to stop the hemorrhage of congregational vitality and mission. Most smaller congregations do not have the membership or financial resources to make such a move possible. They especially find their futures to be vulnerable. This situation underscores the need for a new vision for the ways congregations go about their educational ministries.

These five clues to flaws in church educational structures and strategies permeate the experience of congregations across the United States and Canada. They take different forms in each congregation. Some are more serious than others. And in some congregations local concerns may have more influence on the future effectiveness of church education than any one of these five. The potential in a congregation's education to sustain and renew its identity and mission for the future, however, depends on the extent to which each congregation is able to identify and address the influence of these flaws on their corporate life.

EXERCISE IN CONGREGATIONAL ANALYSIS

Take a sheet of paper and draw a large circle like the one following. Identify five sections with the flaws mentioned above. List clues to those flaws in your own congregation's educational efforts. In the sixth section of the chart write in other flaws you can identify in your congregation's education. In the space on the page outside the circle, list strengths in your congregation's education that counter the influence of these flaws. Save this chart for use with "A Guide to Revisioning Local Church Education."

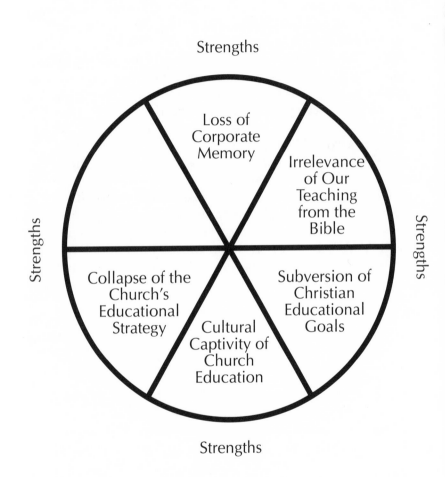

2.

Events that
Form and Transform

DURING THE NINETEENTH CENTURY, Protestant
and Catholic churches turned to the school as the primary agency for the formal task of educating children
and youth into their faith communities. Additional
instruction in the home, other contexts of congregational life, public schools, and other community organizations reinforced the teaching of church schools. During the past fifty years, however, family and community
involvement in the religious education of children and
youth has diminished significantly. Few families read the
Bible or engage in devotional practices in a disciplined
or sustained fashion. Public schools no longer include
prayer, religious celebrations, Bible reading, or explicitly
Christian moral instruction in their daily schedules.
These changes led church leaders to expand their expectations of the church schools—both Sunday and weekday
schools—in teaching moral and religious values, concepts, and practices during the 1950s and 1960s. But
increasing numbers of people soon discovered that the
church's school could not effectively fulfill the full range
of educational functions needed by local congregations
to maintain and renew themselves. Indeed, these additional responsibilities only intensified the diminishing
effectiveness of the church's school in transmitting and
interpreting church traditions. Therefore to revision the

church's education calls for the imaginative apprehension of an alternative guiding image for the task.

One source for that image may be found in the "eventfull" character of the Christian gospel that calls Christian community into existence. The gospel originated in acts of God experienced as events by communities of people. Robert McAfee Brown has observed that all discussions of faith have some relationship to certain events in the past.[1] This includes those discussions among Christians. Something happened long ago in the life, death, and resurrection of Jesus Christ that transformed perspectives, commitments, and ways of living among a small band of people in a small Mediterranean country. The stories of that event have gathered people into its possibilities for centuries, shaping and transforming their lives and culminating in communities of memory and transformation.

Subsequent events—including the Councils of Chalcedon and Nicea, the founding of the Benedictine order, Galileo's scientific discoveries, the nurture of women's spirituality in monastic and pietist settings, Martin Luther's challenge of the medieval practice of indulgences, the establishment of a Puritan Christian commonwealth, John Wesley's Aldersgate experience, and Sojourner Truth's quest for the freedom of slaves, among many others—refine and particularize the meanings of incarnation in our own times and places. Events in our congregations and local communities further refine and focus our faith experience.

Our relationship to these communal events has an educative character. If they are to become important to us, we must be familiar with them. If we are to participate in them, we must learn how to do so. If we are to be agents of their meanings, we must develop sensibilities for the roles and responsibilities needed to fulfill that task. As we try to understand these events we begin to link ideas and actions, to discover new possibilities for living. As these events become increasingly important to us, we find ourselves developing skills to interpret other experiences through their categories and concepts. As we encounter their limits to be gospel in our ever-changing situation, we find ourselves searching for new insights to live into their meanings and out of their possibilities. As we enter into the practice of participating in these events, in other words, they begin to inform and shape who we are.

We begin to identify with them. We take on their character. We discover in them sources to commitments distinguishing us from people who identify with the values, perspectives, and norms of other events. We discover ourselves in a community of people identified with that event. We begin to see the world through the perspectives of the community originating in and shaped by that event. In a paraphrase of the apostle Paul, for those of us who find meaning in the Christ-event, we not only take on the mind and life-style of Christ, we also do so in forms shaped by Luther, Calvin, and other significant figures and communities of faith in our past. These events not only tell us who we are but also to whom we belong. They provide us with clues about how we are to relate to others and to participate in the world around us.

Congregational life is shaped around the ways it remembers certain events. Three quite different experiences have contributed to my growing awareness of the formative power of ancient and recent events in our lives. The first has been the overwhelming adoption of the liturgical calendar in the worship of many so-called non-liturgical Protestant denominations during the past twenty-five years. This has to account for one of the most amazing transformations in Protestant congregational life in the modern era.

When I was a child anything that hinted at the flow of

the liturgical seasons was considered "popish" or "ritualistic" (a judgmental euphemism for anything Roman Catholic and thereby contrary to the perceived "freedom" of Protestant worship). Yet in 1964 when we introduced the Advent wreath, Ash Wednesday service, and the use of liturgical colors into the life of the congregation I served, no one protested. Why? I often wondered. But I think I now have a clue.

As Roman Catholics, Anglicans, and Orthodox Christians have long known, the liturgical seasons provide a structure for the continuing rehearsal of the primary stories of the Christian community. Their rhythmic repetition over time regularly renews our consciousness of those stories at a time in history when we are bombarded with a host of competing stories for our loyalty. The liturgical seasons help us to remember who we are in an era of flux and change. They order the way we live together in relation to the flow of events that remind us of our relationship to the Christ-event. Ultimately they intensify our relationship to one another as we share together liturgical acts of remembering.

A second set of experiences also heightened my awareness to the importance of organizing congregational education around the central events of church life. Those of us whose ancestries are rooted in the traditions of Europe rarely are conscious of the diversity of educational strategies to be found in other cultures. So we have a difficult time envisioning an alternative to the church's education that does not center upon the school or some catechetical process. Many African American congregations, among others, suggest lively alternatives.[2]

African American congregations throughout their history have faced a problem. How does a community of faith maintain and renew its distinctive cultural faith heritage in a society bent on oppressing—even obliterating—that heritage? Although African American churches have long valued the importance of the school to equip its children and youth for a multiracial society, they have also been suspicious of the school as a primary source to building community. Curriculum resources, school organizations, and teacher training procedures could too easily be controlled by the dominant European American population. We see in the heritage of African American congregations consequently an event-centered education.

Through the Exodus of the children of Israel and the Resurrection of Jesus Christ, African Americans discovered a way to become disciples of Christ out of the traditions of Africa. Sunday morning worship embodied and reenacted the eventful amalgam of those stories. Each Sunday rehearsed the liberative content of those stories. Families reinforced and supported the storytelling, Bible reading, and character formation of the church. The power of this education cannot be overestimated. It sustained people through unbelievable trouble and tribulation. It maintained community vitality in the face of the forces of marginalization and oppression. It equipped people to live faithfully in a hostile world.[3]

A third insight into the potential of an event-centered education may be discerned in the experience of many small membership congregations. The dominant educational strategy in these congregations is similar to the unconscious strategies families and kinfolk use to introduce the next generation into their corporate identity. Certain events provide educational opportunities to intensify and renew that identity and to clarify how that community relates to its larger religious and social context. Christmas, Easter, Homecoming, and Mother's Day are common events requiring extensive preparation on the part of the total membership. An intergenerational effort focuses on preparing the total congregation for those events. In their experience we see the transmission of traditions and stories in the shared efforts of old and young directed to the event that orders their common life.

These three insights provide clues to an education that might be responsive to the needs of religious communities in a pluralistic and rapidly changing society. But the experience of these religious communities cannot simply be adopted by others. The pluralism of values, the popular appeal of competing social and political events ranging from July 4th celebrations to the Superbowl, and population mobility call even these groups to reassess and revision their education.

EXERCISE IN CONGREGATIONAL ANALYSIS

Take a large sheet of paper (newsprint or shelf paper will do). Divide it into twelve columns. At the top of each column write in the name of the months.

Review the life of your congregation over the past year to identify those events central to the congregation's worship and mission. Place these events in the proper order in the monthly columns.

You may want to share with one another stories of the influence of these events on your life and faith. Save this chart. We will come back to it later in this chapter.

FORMATIVE EVENTS

Several years ago I participated in a planning retreat for the officers of our local church. One of the pastors began the first session by asking us what had been the most significant parts of the church's ministry during the past year. A young man started the brainstorming process with "baptism." Another person added "holy communion." Another person mentioned Pentecost Sunday. Others expanded the list to include teaching children in vacation church school, Christmas Eve worship, Sunday morning worship, congregational support received during an illness, the fellowship among those who struggled to repair a recurring roof leak, a task force on improving race relations. The process picked up until several sheets of newsprint were covered. The time passed quickly as people shared stories about the influence of these events on their relationships with others and God, the changes these events prompted in their lives, and the hopes and meanings they had derived from their experiences.

As I have thought about this and similar meetings of church administrative councils, the "event-full" character of people's responses became increasingly evident. Despite our usual attention to maintaining the administrative, liturgical, educational, and missional structures in order to keep congregations alive from week to week, those efforts became truly significant only when they provided the framework for events through which we encounter ourselves, others, and the mystery of God in transformational ways. In the possibilities emerging from these encounters we may begin to discover the character of an event-full education.

Discovering the educational potential in the events that order congregational life and nurture congregational faith begins by distinguishing among them. At least four kinds of events provide a rhythmic pattern to the participation of people in communities of all kinds: paradigmatic events, seasonal events, occasional events, and unexpected events.

Paradigmatic events establish a pattern for our lives as persons and as groups. The patterns for Christian life and community have their origin in significant events deeply rooted in our ancient traditions and rituals and recounted in sacred texts and stories. These events provide a persistent structure that gives order and purpose to our common lives. They establish standards and expectations for our participation and commitments. They govern our relationships and inform our sense of mission. And as a vision for community they provide a persistent impetus to the renewal and/or transformation of our common life.

In some churches, especially those in the Reformed church tradition, the stories of covenant events establish that paradigmatic structure and expectation for community in each congregation. In many African American congregations the stories of the Exodus establish a pattern of liberation from bondage that gives meaning and purpose to congregational identity. In other congregations and denominations stories of servanthood or Pentecost provide a common vision for what it means to live as communities of faith. Many people are now discovering in the stories of Hagar, Dorcas, Miriam, and Esther new possibilities for ecclesial life in women's religious experience. These stories stand alongside and incorporate stories of redemptive love, messianic banquets, encounters with strangers, and peaceable kingdoms that also make up our communal traditions.

The significance and meaning of these paradigmatic stories are influenced by the particular histories of given communities of faith. In some congregations the stories of the gospel's paradigmatic events are shaped by the experiences of cultural dominance, in others by a history of conquest, and in others by the pain of slavery. Other congregations are distinguished by the influence of the thinking of Thomas Aquinas, the reflections of Martin Luther, or the spirituality of Lady Julian of Norwich. Expectations for community in other congregations may be shaped by patterns of piety. We see this at work in those communities of faith influenced by the rule of Benedict and the disciplines of John and Charles Wesley. The unfolding of these meanings of paradigmatic events over time helps sustain and renew congregational perceptions and life-styles.

These meanings are reflected in metaphors congregations use to identify themselves: the people of the Cross; ambassadors for Christ; the fellowship of reconciliation; Presbyterians; Baptists; a Bible-believing church. Their significance is maintained in the stories and rituals of the congregation that remind and renew the relationship of its members to the power of those events.

Seasonal events rhythmically pattern the life of congregations. The ritual processes that structure these events carry congregations through the liturgical seasons from Advent through Christmas, Epiphany, Lent, Easter, and Pentecost, through the calendar of saints' days, and through local seasons ranging from Homecoming Sunday to the annual revival. These seasonal events establish a structure for the interplay of a congregation's identification with certain paradigmatic events in our faith history and its responses over the years to local circumstances and relationships. These events provide the clearest and most consistent structure for the education of a congregation. They provide a regular ordering of congregational life for weekly worship, study, mission, and fellowship. Seasonal events, however, have little power in the lives of people if they are not familiar with the texts and ritual actions that sustain them.

Occasional events intensify community identity and mission, illuminate community meanings, and energize community life. These events include weddings, funerals, baptisms, anniversaries, mission trips, and church building dedications. We see their power in the heightened attention and focused energy of a congregation whenever a young couple brings a child before the congregation to be baptized or dedicated. In the ebb and flow of these occasional events, congregational identity and mission are intensified and renewed.

Again the participation of people in these events is heightened and the significance of these events is enhanced when people prepare to participate in them. Many congregations develop educational processes to prepare persons for baptism and confirmation. Church membership is preceded by an orientation series. Premarital "counseling" precedes a wedding. A work camp usually involves a time for orientation and planning before it takes place. Election to a position of leadership requires a period of training. Although these educational activities are often viewed as perfunctory, they have the potential to intensify and focus the faith journeys of persons and groups. Their contribution to the nurture of congregational identity and mission cannot be overestimated.

Unexpected events intrude into the lives of congregations. They interrupt the rhythmic patterns, structures, and relationships that have given coherence and order to the way congregations function. These unexpected events bring joy and sorrow, blessing and suffering. They come in many forms—a tragedy in the life of a church member or the community at large, a changing population in the church and neighborhood, a fire in the church building, the establishment or the closing of a major industry, the request of a homeless person for assistance, a congregational conflict, a generous bequest, the presence of strangers in worship, the birth of a child with a serious disability, the decline in price supports for a basic agricultural product, among a myriad of other possibilities.

These unexpected events cut across traditional program divisions. They influence people of all ages. They challenge the community's experience and interpretation of the central stories of its faith. They may become the impetus to new ways of understanding and responding to the intent of those stories. In this instance education emerges from the responses of a congregation. It becomes an occasion for making meaning out of that which was not expected. The education surrounding these unexpected events often has a spontaneous and informal structure. It occurs in response to an immediate need. It may last no more than a few moments during a phone call or pastoral visit. It may be a comprehensive and planned response involving a significant block of time in the life of a congregation. In whatever form it takes, the character of the education responsive to the unexpected events in congregational life is shaped by the event itself.

The education of a community around the events that give structure and momentum to its life involves three movements. I have already indicated what they are. They require **preparation** to empower our participation. The goal is to move from ignorance, incompetence, and naïveté to familiarity and finally to the competence required for free and full participation in worship and mission. Ignorance and lack of familiarity with any event only creates alienation, powerlessness, and hostility.

Adequate preparation for participation in the events of common life cannot be assumed. It requires developing enough *familiarity* with the stories, texts, roles, and actions associated with a given event that people can engage them without feeling awkward or out of place. It requires enough *practice* that participants can unselfconsciously anticipate experiencing something of the power the event has had for people in the past. It requires rigorous *examination* of the texts, symbols, and actions identified with the event to discover in their experience of the event new meanings and perspectives for living into the changing circumstances of each new day.

The second movement in event-full education involves our **engagement** in the event. Events transform lives only as people enter into them and allow their imaginations to be filled with its possibilities, their relationships with its expectations, and their practices with its values. Repeated engagement with the meanings and practices of certain events help embed us in their emerging possibilities. A lack of engagement reduces us to the passivity of observation without calling us to commitment or transformation. The necessity of engagement in learning is reflected in the popular wisdom that one learns best by doing.

Event-full education comes full circle with **mutually critical reflection** on the meanings people draw from their engagement with the event. This phase of the educational process is crucial if the meanings of the event are to be useful to us outside the boundaries of the event, if the event is to make any lasting difference in our efforts to be faithful in the social, political, economic, and interpersonal maelstrom that makes up contemporary living. Mutually critical reflection requires *sharing* our experience of the events in which we participate; that is, to tell our own story as a part of the greater story we engaged. It necessitates *assessing* meanings we draw from that engagement from the perspective of our faith traditions, the biblical witness, and the experience of people who draw different meanings from their own engagement in the event. Mutually critical reflection becomes transformational when we begin to live out of our commitment to the meanings we have discovered. At this point we may begin to take on or incarnate the meanings of the event. Our lives are illumined and focused by the repetition of our preparation, engagement, and critical reflection on the event.

The structure of an event-full education is not complex, but if taken seriously, it could radically alter the way congregations order their educational ministries. Its emphases would include at least the following:

1. Congregational education would focus primarily on two tasks. The first would be to empower the participation of children, youth, and adults in worship and mission, the central actions of the church. The second would be to increase the ability of children, youth, and adults to reflect critically on the meanings of their participation in worship and mission for the sake of their commitment to and involvement in God's transformation of the world.

2. Curriculum resources in congregational education would be designed to facilitate the knowledge and skills necessary to the participation and critical reflection of children, youth, and adults in worship and mission.

3. Event-full education would occur wherever and whenever teachers and leaders with gifts, graces, skills, and sensitivities appropriate to the educational efforts of preparation and critical reflection facilitate the learning of children, youth, and adults.

4. Event-full education would occur whenever and wherever people of the congregation can be most efficiently gathered to prepare for and to reflect on their participation in worship and mission.

5. Event-full education would occur whenever and wherever attention is given to the disciplined and orderly involvement of children, youth, and adults in occasions for teaching and learning that prepare them to participate in or reflect critically on events that call them into the transformational activity of God. Some congregations may appropriate or adapt existing educational agencies—Sunday schools, after school programs, Saturday schools, choir programs, evening recreation programs, and long-term disciplined educational processes such as RCIA in the Roman Catholic Church or Disciple Bible Studies in The United Methodist Church—to equip peo-

ple for participation in and reflection on their encounters with the holy in congregational events of worship and mission. Other congregations will create new structures and design new educational processes to provide optimal opportunities for the teaching and learning of its members.

EXERCISE IN CONGREGATIONAL ANALYSIS

Return to the chart of events you just created. Take three color markers or crayons. Circle all repeated seasonal events in one color, all occasional events in a second color, and all unexpected events in a third color.

Choose two or three different kinds of events from each list. Identify and list when and how people are prepared to participate in them. Repeat the process to locate when and how people reflect critically on the meanings of these events for their lives.

To what extent do these educational activities help the members of your congregation participate competently in these events?

Is there a biblical story, theological concept, or historical event that illumines the identity and mission of your congregation? If so, explore in what ways the life of your congregation illustrates the content of this "paradigmatic event."

Save this information to review again in "A Guide to Revisioning Local Church Education."

3.

Building Community

AS A TEENAGER I LEARNED a song at church camp that continues to be popular in many church youth groups.

> I'm goin'a sing when the Spirit says sing,
> I'm goin'a sing when the Spirit says sing,
> I'm goin'a sing when the Spirit says sing,
> And obey the Spirit of the Lord.[1]

Other verses focus on acts of prayer and praise. The song illumines a problem for a Christian community confronting the increasing faith illiteracy in our churches. How can we sing if we do not know the words and tunes? How can we pray if do not know the stories of God's mysterious and unconventional engagement with humanity? How can we shout if we are not familiar with words of praise? Perhaps the significance of these questions will become apparent through the story of an event in the life of one congregation.

"IT'S THE ONLY STORY THEY KNOW"

For several years our family participated in a "cathedral church." It stands on a busy street opposite a major university and not far from the urban center of a mid-size metropolitan city. The church building looks like a

51

cathedral. Its size and English Gothic architecture evoke a sense of awe and reverence. It provides a dramatic setting for worship. The quality of music, the sensitivity of the liturgists to the rhythms and nuances of the spoken word, and the power of the preaching heighten the drama of worship. On Sunday mornings people arrive early to find a seat. Unlike most worshiping Protestant congregations, the first seats to fill are those nearest the pulpit and altar table.

One of the most popular liturgical events in this congregation occurs at 11:00 P.M. on Christmas Eve. Some people arrive early. Simple decorations heighten the dramatic play of light across the stone arches. Trees decorated with tiny white lights illuminate the chancel area. The choir sings. The Christmas story is told. The Eucharist is celebrated. Those gathering for this event include a diverse cross section of the city. Many, of course, "belong" to this congregation. Several children can be seen scattered here and there across the sanctuary, but most had participated in an earlier worship service. The teenagers participate in force. This liturgical event has become an important shared experience for them over the years. As usual they sit together in the balcony.

Many strangers find their way to that worship service. They are a diverse group. Some are young adults. Some arrive in expensive cars and wear clothes of the latest fashion. Some are often seen in the homeless shelters of the city. When I asked the senior minister where they come from, he told me most of the unfamiliar faces are not members of the church. Most come only on Christmas Eve. Most prefer anonymity. When I asked why they come, his reply surprised me: "It is the only story they know."

The more I ponder his answer to my question, the more it influences my understanding of the church's educational mission. Initially it called into question the way I often criticized people who participated in worship only on Christmas and Easter. Later his words filled me with the urgency of the hope in that congregation's unexpected guests. The awkwardness of their participation had blinded me to their hunger for some connection to the mystery of holiness. Eventually I realized their presence probably had more in common with the visit of the shepherds and wise men to an ancient manger stall than did my own habitual attendance. They were seeking an intimate moment with the mystery of God.

Why did they come? Perhaps they came because at some point in their lives they had heard a promise in the stories and songs of the Incarnation. Perhaps they still possessed a rudimentary vocabulary of faith, a memory that on this evening people gathered to celebrate the mystery of God's presence. Maybe they had reached some point in their lives when those memories kindled some hope—that if they could hear once again that ancient story they might experience a saving word, a reconciling word, a healing word to transform the pain, boredom, or loneliness in their lives.

The dilemma, of course, is that given the current practices in Christian education this group of Christmas Eve worshipers may not be present in the future. The reasons are clear. Few congregations gather the majority of their membership into extended rehearsals of the sacred events that give form and purpose to their lives. Instead, congregational life, even in many small churches, invites people to observe re-enactments of its central events. Congregations no longer organize their lives to ensure familiarity with the sacred texts of the Christian heritage among their members. Instead they are read or sung for the most part, only on their appointed lectionary Sundays. Public schools no longer produce Christmas plays and concerts. The carols of Christmas and Easter are not sung at the beginning of the school day. The media scrambles sacred and secular songs to the point that messages of incarnation and economic exploitation jumble in our minds. Consequently, for great numbers of people, the birth of Christ has more to do with economic well-being than with peace and justice. And in comparison with Christmas, the rest of the church's holy days only exist on the periphery of public consciousness.

Church education is out of touch with the diminishing effects of its efforts.[2] With each generation over the past fifty years, attrition in knowledge and skills crucial to a corporate Christian witness has relentlessly sapped the strength of the church's identity and mission. Congregations engage primarily in an education that ensures the increase of their ignorance and the intensification of the powerlessness of their members. This does not mean we are not engaged in educational activities. Church members spend much time and energy organizing and supervising educational programs. But their efforts do not deter the pervading ignorance shaping congregational life.

Ignorance is a terrible thing. It destroys the bonds linking generations. The capacity of youth to see in the visions of their elders possibilities for their own future diminishes. The importance of elders discerning in the commitments of the young extensions of their own hopes dissipates. Ignorance diminishes community identity and purpose. It causes people to confuse religious experience with faith knowledge by thirsting after the former and resisting the latter. It subjects the authority of the traditions of faith and scripture to personal experience. It paradoxically resists the possibility that God might still speak through new voices and in "strange" places and simultaneously accepts as authoritative voices contradicting historic messages of love and justice. Ultimately ignorance can lead to the extinction of a community. Ignorance prevents us from discovering who we are and to whom we belong.

EXERCISE IN CONGREGATIONAL ANALYSIS

Complete the following questionnaire to begin to identify the extent to which the problem of ignorance is present in your congregation. After completing the questionnaire identify implications from your answers for the future of your congregation.

COMMUNITY INVENTORY IDENTITY

1. List stories from the Bible and church tradition the high school seniors in your congregation or parish could tell without prompting.

2. List hymns the high school seniors could sing from memory. How many of these are choruses?

3. What beliefs, religious practices, and life-style commitments would high school seniors in your congregation identify as distinctive to your denominational heritage and identity?

4. List prayers they could say by memory.

5. Identify women and men (other than Jesus) from biblical and church history the seniors in high school you know would identify as exemplary models for their own faith journeys.

6. List the creeds and other parts of the liturgy of the congregation they would know by memory.

LEARNING TO HEAR

If the church is to be the Body of Christ in the world, the primary purpose of the church's education is to "build up" that body—to create communities incarnating

God's love to participate in God's transformation of the
world to emancipate all creation from bondage. The
urgency of that task weighs heavily upon us. The invasive
and destructive forces diminishing the experience and
possibility of any sense of community surround us. The
dynamics of pluralism have shattered the sense of mutuality associated with a common place (seen in the concept of "parish") or common task (as seen in the concept
of a voluntary society) to evoke or create some sense of
mutuality and interdependence.

Perhaps the most powerful of all gifts to the world
found in the Christian heritage is its sense of community.
Its promises confront the messages of fragmentation and
violence dominating social relationships. It breaks
through our finite distinctions of race, culture, age, class,
gender, and ability to celebrate the necessary interdependence of all people. It confronts our human proclivity to argument and dissension in the affirmation that all
of us are children of God. We therefore have "a common
ancestry." We share "a common heritage" originating in
God's creativity and spilling across the ages and through
the nations of humanity. We "have a common experience"—an insight increasingly real to those of us living
into the twenty-first century.[3] A rape in Bosnia, a drought
in Africa, a wheat crop failure in the Ukraine, the relent-
less deforestation along the Amazon or in the Pacific
Northwest affect us all. At the same time the selfless giving of Mother Teresa, the finesse of an Olympic ice
skater, the vision of Martin Luther King, Jr. can inspire us
all. The media declares we live in a "global village." The
interdependence implied in that metaphor, however, has
long been at the heart of the Christian vision of community.

That ancient vision is found in the New Testament
expectations for *koinonia* formed around the life and
mission of Jesus Christ. It stands over against the race

toward human destruction on every front. This means that in a world dangerously imperiled for the lack of a vision for community, the primary social task of the church is, as Stanley Hauerwas who teaches ethics at Duke University has written, to be nothing less than "a community capable of hearing the story of God we find in the scripture and living in a manner that is faithful to that story."[4]

The Bible has a lot to say about "hearing" and about the "living" grounded in our responses to what we hear. Usually it involves more than the exercise of the ear. It emphasizes our appropriation of what we have heard— the extent to which we have heard with heart, mind, and soul. Gospel words can be hard. "This is a hard saying;" Jesus said. "Who can hear it?" (John 6:60 KJV). It calls for change, turnaround, transformation in our relationship to God, others, and the world that is our home.

The dynamics of hearing involve at least three reflective actions.

1. Can we hear what the speaker intends? Do we recognize the words and the possibilities that the speaker's situation and perspective might bring to the message intended for our hearing?

2. Are we clear about what we intend or mean for the words we use in our own efforts to communicate with others?

3. While listening to the "other" and to ourselves, how do we then choose to respond to the "other"?

We can see the interplay of these three movements in hearing in any interpersonal communication. They are especially evident in the candor of our interactions with young children. Do we hear behind the child's sudden hug and words "I love you" to the spontaneous gratitude for the security and well-being experienced in our care? Do we hear the full range of our own intentions when we respond back with "I love you too"? Do we recognize our impatience over the interruption or our tolerance with the intrusion or our joy in the unaffected and unsolicited gift of those words? Our hearing often leads to action. Perhaps it pulls us into a hug; it evokes a tear. It leads us to tell the child to stop bothering us; or it may elicit a shared giggle. In the mutuality of that speaking and hearing we accept responsibility for living out the ethical implications of that child's affirmation of love.

To hear God's word involves a similar process.

1. It begins with intentional listening into the creating Word for a redemptive, graceful, judging word speaking to our condition. Since the meanings associated with words we receive from the past through scripture, story, hymn, prayer, or creed are not fixed, they fall on our listening ears—if we are attentive—with new possibility, new significance.

2. It continues as we listen to the thoughts and words we use to address God. If we "hear" God, God's words confront us with what we bring to this relationship. Is it similar to the awe of Isaiah before the Holy of Holies in the temple? the confidence of Esther in an encounter over the future of her people? the apprehension of Moses before the burning bush? the fear of Peter in a crowded courtyard? In the reciprocity of our hearing and speaking with God our listening calls us beyond the physical act of the ear into the possibilities of our hearing.

3. We now come to the third dynamic in the act of "hearing" in our response to the content of our hearing. When we respond to the new possibilities discerned from our hearing, we find ourselves caught up in the mutuality of God's intent for relating to humankind. We discover that our hearing calls us to participate in God's quest for the emancipation of creation. The activity of hearing led Moses to Pharaoh, Jeremiah to the king of Judah, Mary to a very unusual motherhood, Paul to a lifetime of missionary activity. Our own hearing will lead

into responses filled with the liveliness of God's intent for the world and all who dwell in it.

For anyone who has read the prophetic writings and the Psalms, the biblical command "to hear" is familiar. But for those of us living out of predominantly visual ways of knowing and being, the dynamics involved in hearing in education may come as something of a shock. The schools of the church (Sunday school, C.C.D., catechism classes, preschool, after school and day school programs) have for the most part emphasized patterns of learning based on seeing rather than hearing. Clarence Joseph Rivers, who helped introduce African American liturgical experience into Roman Catholic worship, has pointed out that learning based on seeing "is geared to perceive the continuing line" on the printed page, in the flow of a mathematical problem, or in the organization of a research paper. It "fosters a perception of a world in which one thing is connected with the other, whether in fact it is connected or not. It abhors suddenness and discontinuity." It focuses on "one thing at a time." It emphasizes "the particular and abstracts it" from its context. It lies behind the quest to distinguish, analyze, categorize, "to separate things that in reality are not separate." It seeks detachment rather than engagement.[5]

Learning based primarily on the capacity to see has contributed much to human history. Its influence is evident in the emphasis on linear and sequential logic in the thinking of theologians, philosophers, and lawyers through much of western history. It undergirds the scientific quest to understand the whole by analyzing its parts—a quest that led to the industrial and technological revolutions. It establishes the categories upon which the efficient processes of industrial and governmental and even ecclesiastical bureaucracies are built. It informs the organization of curriculum resource designs that arrange the content to be taught into manageable and sequential units. It informs our commitment to the worth of the individual person in society. But there are other values in the human community.

An education that relies on hearing emphasizes the interdependence, mutuality, and interconnectedness of experience. We can see these dynamics at work whenever two people are speaking and listening to each other. If we want to hear another person, we lean in toward that person. We lose our detachment. We slip into a pattern of rhythmic interaction linking us together in the give and take of communication. In his studies of these communication patterns, anthropologist Edward Hall has compared the actions of people engaged in speaking and hearing to a dance. As people speak and listen to each other, they move through a variety of tempos and rhythms as if their interactions had been choreographed. In this dance we are bound in relationship with the other.[6] We cannot exist without the other.

Formal education in the churches in North America has emphasized visual learning almost exclusively. Many of our church people do not have the listening skills that lie at the heart of our congregational efforts to create communities of faith responsive to God and the people around them. I am reminded of several adult Bible classes I have known through the years. Although class members have gathered weekly for years, sitting in rows, and reading Bible passages verse by verse, they only know one another superficially. Even worse, they often have no clue to the deeper messages of the words they have been reading. Their attention has been directed to obvious and often superficial information. They have dissected a text, but have never moved deeper than the meaning of the words to listen for the centuries of responsiveness of people to God through those words. Such classes often become doctrinaire and inflexible. They see and read the words, but have difficulty hearing God's creating and redeeming Word through them. They have accumulated information by "banking" it in the storehouses of their minds, rather than discovering its potential for their own liberation in the Spirit of God.[7]

These thoughts began with a meditation on the meaning of the presence of strangers in a Christmas Eve worship service. Those strangers lead me to wonder if the education in our churches fosters the kind of hearing necessary for building communities of responsive faithfulness. Undoubtedly most congregations have moments of hearing in their educational ministries, moments when people catch glimpses of God's call to mutuality in the quest for the transformation of the world. But I *see* congregations and *hear* in the words of their leaders more concern about recruiting enough volunteer teachers to "cover" all classes, finding non-controversial and simple-to-teach curriculum resources, managing the education program with efficiency and order, ensuring proper behavior of children and youth in church, and attracting the right kind of newcomers to keep church membership growing than with building up communities of faith for a vocation of praise and service in ministries of emancipatory transformation.

EXERCISE IN CONGREGATIONAL ANALYSIS

Where in your congregation are children, youth, and or adults (classes, worship, administrative, missional, or fellowship settings) encouraged to

1. listen for God's intent through the words of scripture, stories, hymns, prayers, or creeds for people in the past and for today?

2. listen for the oft-hidden intentions for themselves, others, the church, the neighborhood of the church, or the world in their own words?
3. listen for clues to ways they might respond to what they hear God calling them to be and to do?

List these times and places. Describe what makes these educational moments and settings different from other educational activities in your congregation. Save this information for use later.

EDUCATIONAL PURPOSES
IN BUILDING COMMUNITY

Three purposes deeply rooted in the processes of hearing and responding to the Word of God may be discerned in the unfolding life of faith communities centered on the event of Jesus Christ. They establish a framework for thinking in new ways about an education capable of building up communities of faith for the nurture of Christian identity and mission. Each purpose is grounded in the reciprocal dynamics of listening and responding.

Walter Brueggemann, an interpreter of Old Testament texts, has identified one purpose for church education integral to the dynamics of the hearing that builds community. Church education *binds the generations* into community. In the congregation's elders, those who are young in age and faith discover clues to the meaning and power of events central to the identity and mission of the church. Through the youth of the congregation, the elders envision the community's continuity and renewal. If church education is not intensely intergenerational, the "continuity" of its "vision, value, and perception" cannot be maintained over time or renewed for changing circumstances.[8]

Through the elders of the congregation and the saints of the faith tradition, church education introduces people into the communal memory of the church. Memory is central to the vitality of any community. It is the repository of the community's past. It links events across the community's history into a web of meanings that in turn, embed us in their perception and promise. Through memory we live into and are shaped by those events that distinctively shape the life and mission of a community. We live out of those events and extend their meanings into yet another generation. Despite the centuries separating us, we live as brothers and sisters with Miriam, Moses and Aaron, the prophets, Mary Magdalene and Peter, Paul and Dorcas, Augustine and Catherine, Luther and Wesley, Dorothy Day and Sophie Fahs.

The function of memory is not to pull us into the past. It beckons us instead to embrace a future originating in events that called our communities into being. It fuels the efforts of communities to live with hope into the future. It gives impetus to community creativity and transformation, to freedom and new life.[9] It builds on the dialogical yearning of children to know to whom they belong and on the passion of the community's elders to share the wisdom and values integral to that belonging.

The dynamic of binding generations is not simply the imparting of the wisdom of the elders to the young. It occurs whenever the experiences of life thrust any of us into a new naïveté, a new period of questioning and doubt, a new time of uncertainty and confusion, a new period of pain and suffering, or a time of new challenges and possibilities. In these moments we seek out the compassion, insight, and wisdom, not only of our immediate elders, but also of the saints of our community's past. We search through their experience, not for their answers to the issues and questions they faced but for clues to God's promises for the future. That effort heightens our consciousness of the relationships we have with those from the past who brought us to this place and time. We are also made aware of those in the future, whose anticipation of God's transforming word is dependent, in part, on the faithfulness with which we read the texts, tell the stories, sing the songs, and pray the prayers inherited from our faith ancestors. The task of building up communities of faith requires constant attention to nurturing these historical relationships.

In building community a second purpose of church education is to *nurture partnership* among the members of the community. In the context of the unfolding of the Christ-event, partnership means something quite different from the legal contract of two or more persons establishing a business proposition. It has to do with the quality and character of our relationships with one another.

Letty Russell, whose theological writings grew out of her pastoral experience in East Harlem, has suggested that our English word *partnership* most effectively translates the intent of the Greek word *koinonia*.[10] The images of the quality of common life found in partnership in the New Testament are many. The account of Pentecost celebrates the experience of intimacy embracing the diversity of language and culture. Eucharistic narratives such as the feeding of the five thousand challenge contemporary tendencies to limit intimacy to the gathering of two or three persons in Christ's name. Paul's repeated emphasis upon the interdependence of the members of the community challenges our preoccupation with the organizational life of congregations. The mutuality envisioned in being the Body of Christ reveals a shared responsiveness to the pain of economic disparity and injustice just as much as it does to the pain of a serious illness or the death of a loved one. The dynamics of reciprocal mutuality permeate the expectations of the church as *koinonia*.

Sharon Welch points out that partnership moves us beyond consensus strategies for building community to the solidarity of community. In consensus some voices acquiesce to the power and influence of others to move on with the task at hand or in response to hidden dynamics of power and influence in the life of a group. Partnership in contrast, celebrates diversity and multiplicity. Precedent and power do not receive preferential treatment before God. Instead as signs of God's creativity, our differences (age, ethnicity, race, gender, economic and social status, nationality, and so on) are to be respected and valued for their contributions to our common life. They become the springboard to the reciprocity of affirmation and critique integral to the processes of mutual transformation. Partnership in this regard leads to the power embodied in "empathy and compassion" and in our "delight" in the "otherness" of our neighbors. Our communal strength comes from "the solidarity of listening to others." It is reinforced as we bear one another's stories of pain and suffering and support one another's resistance to oppression and dominance. It emerges from our shared quest for freedom and responsibility rather than for control and obligation.[11]

We often glimpse the solidarity of partnership in the worship of diverse peoples (just as worship is often the most exclusive of Christian corporate action). I think of a suburban congregation during the height of the Viet Nam War on a World Communion Sunday. The pastor of this predominantly middle-class and European American congregation was seeking to create an experience of unity out of that congregation's diversity (or solidarity in partnership), and asked several people to help serve the communion elements. They included a man and a woman, the oldest and the youngest members, a black and a white member, a republican and a democrat activist, a military officer and a pacifist, a liberal and a conservative, among others. Strange as it may seem, this act of underscoring human differences in this most intensely communal moment in Christian life reinforced the sense of mutuality among this congregation's members. Solidarity of our relatedness, in other words, becomes most real in the affirmation and celebration of differences.

A third purpose for building community through the church's education *links strangers* as neighbors. Letty Russell, Parker Palmer, Henri Nouwen, and others have already made this point. Church education involves its members in the practice of hospitality. This ancient biblical response to the presence of the stranger creates places of shalom for people to enter into respectful conversation across their differences, to give and receive gifts that have the potential of transforming one another's experience.

Much of the biblical attention to hospitality provided guidance for ways of relating to strangers "in our midst." The assumption of course, was that these neighbors from outside the family, tribe, or nation would soon leave. The rules of hospitality consequently focused on the development of attitudes and behaviors appropriate to momentary mutuality.

Our contemporary situation complicates patterns of sociability originating in ancient Jerusalem, Antioch, or Rome. Our cities and towns—indeed, many of our congregations—are not made up of "our kind of people" whatever we may define that group to be. We live instead, in the midst of a plurality of strangers. In this situation the dynamics of hospitality shift. Although we may continue to take the stranger into our homes and churches, the greater responsibility is to incarnate hospitality in a hostile world. We are called to engage in an education that embodies openness to the presence of God in the swirl of the strangers around us.

Henri Nouwen poignantly captures the essence of this educational task for our churches.

Hospitality . . . means primarily the creation of a free space where the stranger can enter and become a friend instead of an enemy. Hospitality is not to change people, but to offer them space where change can take place. It is not to bring men and women over to our side, but to offer freedom not disturbed by dividing lines. It is not to lead our neighbor into a corner where there are no alternatives left, but to open a wide spectrum of options for choice and commitment.[12]

The kind of hospitality that Nouwen advocates does not promote a passivity on the part of anyone. Instead it requires the kind of attentive listening that enables each to hear beneath the words the other speaks. This kind of hearing involves both a receptivity that accepts the stranger "into our world on his or her terms, not on ours." But it also involves "confrontation" as we each define the boundaries through which we orient ourselves to the worlds of the others and by which we make clear what we bring to the relationship that might emerge from our encounters.[13]

EXERCISE IN CONGREGATIONAL ANALYSIS

Review the list of events in your congregation that you created after reading chapter 2.

Which events effectively bind the generations in your congregation?

Which create patterns of partnership among people typically separated from one another by age, gender, ethnicity, social class, professional occupations, or something else?

Which nurtures hospitality for strangers in and beyond the life of your congregation?

Which hinder the building of community among church members?

EDUCATIONAL TASKS
IN BUILDING COMMUNITY

Community does not just happen. It requires the commitment and effort of its members to intend that its future shall be maintained and renewed through subsequent generations. During the nineteenth century Protestant and Catholic church leaders sought a uniform strategy for congregational education. We live in an era with quite different expectations. Organizations and communities seek an education capable of both extending their distinctive values and life-style into the future and equipping their adherents to live creatively in a pluralistic world. Unlike educational theorists of the last century, we cannot assume a single strategy will be appropriate to all congregations, denominations, or religions. Instead, every congregation is charged with the responsibility of creating community in its own context.

For Christian communities of faith, the organizing principle for building community emerges from their relationship to the events that give purpose and meaning to their existence. It leads to an education equipping people to participate with body, mind, and soul in acts of praise and service—the two distinguishing responses of Christians to the transformational work of God in the world. An education based on this principle emphasizes at least four tasks pertinent to building community in a pluralistic world: (1) transmitting the vocabulary of Christian faith; (2) sharing the stories of faith; (3) nurturing interdependent relationships; and (4) practicing the life-style of Christian community.

Transmitting the Vocabulary of Christian Community. One Sunday morning the pastor of a congregation I was visiting stopped in the middle of her sermon. She leaned over the pulpit and said, "Now I want all of the children to listen carefully to me." She, of course, had the undivided attention of everyone. She then proceeded to define and clarify a concept she was exploring in the sermon. Repeatedly in my visits to this church I noticed that she and several lay leaders would stop children or youth in whatever they were doing to define a term, reinforce a value, or suggest an alternative behavior. I always experienced the interaction as an affirmation rather than a reprimand.

This congregation seems to understand implicitly at least that no community can survive if its members do not have a common vocabulary to communicate its deepest commitments and meanings. Christian communities have rich and complex vocabularies. They consist of words, signs, images, symbols, and rhythms. These building blocks to communication are clustered into spoken, sung, and enacted messages. The vocabularies of Christian communities originated in the interaction of God and people at specific times and places. Through the centuries, the stories, poems, songs, and dances evoking these events have received overlays of meanings nuanced by the subsequent experience of people whose lives have been shaped by them. Thus one Christian community is often distinguished from another, as in Roman Catholic, Greek Orthodox, various Protestant denominations, as well as between two congregations with the same theological heritage within the same community.

In the flow of sacred and mundane time these shared events create a cradle of experience—much of it unconscious until its threatened loss makes us aware of it. The process is similar to the experience of the swimmer whose consciousness of our human dependence on air is most clear just prior to breaking out of the water to gasp another breath.

This corporate vocabulary distinguishes one community from another. We can tell a person from France from a person from Germany not so much by looking at them, but by hearing them. We can also distinguish between Christians and Buddhists on the basis of religious languages—even when their conversation is in English. If we listen carefully we can also tell the difference between Episcopalians and Baptists and between the members of the Foster household and the Smith household. We also recognize distinctive cultural nonverbal vocabularies—the handshake and finger pointing of many European Americans and the bow and the slight head nodding of many Asians; the kneeling in prayer of Roman Catholics and the standing in prayer among Presbyterians. When we hear a set of drums it does not take us long to know whether they reflect music originating in Africa, Argentina, Mexico, or Northern Europe.

Our faith vocabularies do more than shape our perceptions. They inform our sense of who we are. If we do not know the words associated with the sacred texts found in scripture, creeds, prayers, and hymns integral to our particular as well as general Christian church traditions, we cannot live out of the promises of the Christian story. If we do not know the sounds of joy and sorrow, confession and forgiveness, we cannot sing the hymns of praise and service distinguishing the faith of our ancestors. If we do not know the historic rhythms of interactions between God and the people of God, then we cannot gather in corporate acts of praise and service growing out of the responsiveness of Abraham and Sarah centuries ago. In an era when a cacophony of languages competes for our commitment and loyalty, the urgency of immersing ourselves in the Christian language weighs heavily upon us.

Sharing Stories of Faith. In one sense the story of Christian faith is an integral part of the church's vocabularies. But its contribution to building community must be highlighted. In recent years, many people in the church have recognized the dangers of an education that overvalues rationalistic approaches to the study of faith and have called for a re-appropriation of the centrality of story. Walter Brueggemann underscores the point. "The primal mode of education in the church," he has written, "is story—especially any education that takes the formative power of the *Torah* seriously. Trouble surfaces in the community of faith whenever we move from the idiom of story." Whenever we shift our primary attention away from story, "we create an incongruity between our convictions and the ways we speak our convictions." We find ourselves preoccupied with questions that distract us from the primary task of church education—to build communities of faith capable of nurturing our identification with God's transformational mission. The Israelites, Brueggemann continues, knew that if "the story is not believed, nothing added to it" to answer those questions, "will make any difference."[14]

Formal church education in our congregations does not emphasize story. Curriculum resources tell stories. Indeed they are filled with stories. But since they are not repeated often enough to be remembered their function is to convey an idea or moral value or to entertain. Church leaders are usually more interested in the behavior of children and youth than they are in their identification with significant biblical or historical figures or their relationship to the stories of creation and redemption. And everyone seeks religious experience. Although all of these have their place, they overwhelm and diminish the centrality of story in creating and revisioning community life.

At one point in John Steinbeck's *The Winter of our Discontent*, two men are discussing why one persists in attending the worship services of the local Episcopal church. "Let's say that when I was a little baby, and all my bones were soft and malleable, I was put in a small Episcopal cruciform box and so took my shape. Then when I broke out of the box the way a baby chick escapes an egg, is it strange that I had the shape of a cross?"[15] Stories are important because they give purpose and form to our lives. They shape our perceptions and responses.

Young children know how stories should be told. They seek out stories that have the power to fire their imaginations, shape their expectations, and form their behavior. We know the process well. They ask us to read a story. If they like it, they request it over and over again. They do not want the story changed in the slightest. They even reach the point where they live out the story in their play. It helps them make sense of their experience. Note these methods for learning how to hear deeply into the meanings of the community's tradition: repetition, memorization, reinforcement, recitation, imaginative play. These methods are central to telling stories. They are also central to the task of taking on the identity of the people to whom a child belongs.

Too often, however, our storytelling follows the example of mass media. Stories are told once, then discarded. Stories are chosen for their capacity to stimulate and excite, to control or limit, rather than for their potential to create and shape perceptions and values. Stories are told to make a point rather than to open up a world. Should we be surprised then, when children "forget" they have heard a story we have only read to them once or twice? Should we be surprised when they are bored with a story we choose for them only now and then? The challenge to reclaim the power of storytelling is a great one. It requires that children, youth, and adults discover or rediscover the possibilities of God's work in their lives. It also means rekindling the intimacy between the generations in our congregations.[16]

Too often we also have limited the stories we tell to those that perpetuate the values of our people rather than to tell stories that reveal the breadth and depth of

God's perspective on the human experience. We shove to the margins of our consciousness stories that question our motivations, our structures, our political and economic decisions. Some of these stories—especially those of women—have been marginalized for centuries. Only now are we beginning to discover, through a new hearing by women, God's word in the experience of Rachel, Hagar, or in the Syro-Phoenician woman's encounter with Jesus. Latin American base communities have confronted North American and European Christians with their predilections toward biblical and theological narratives of privilege. New Christian communities in Asia and Africa are discovering God's grace in stories of strangers that reverse many of the hierarchical and paternalistic notions of human relating they had learned from Christian missionaries from Europe and North America. Each of these challenges confront us with our tendencies to avoid the whole of the narrative of God's love for humanity. Any faithful telling of stories to build community, however, must include all of God's stories.

Nurturing Relational Interdependence. The most formidable obstacle to building Christian community today may be the preponderance of forces limiting the development of intergenerational and intergroup relationships. Despite people's fascination with Westerhoff's description of the affiliative character of a child's journey of faith, few churches assess the extent to which their worship, education, fellowship, and service intensify the identification of children with the congregation as a community of faith or alienate them from Christian community. Even more intriguing is the lack of attention to his call for congregational environments conducive to the searching faith of adolescents and young adults.[17] Too few congregations provide qualitative relationships embodying the power and possibilities of good news for children, youth, or seeking adults.

Adults today tend to "take care" of children and youth rather than invite them into their lives. A number of years ago Kenneth Keniston and his colleagues observed that parents spend more time managing the people and programs serving their children than anything else. They negotiate with teachers, schedule appointments with doctors and dentists, arrange for music lessons and participation in sports activities, keep their calendars, and chauffeur the children to their many activities. The activities of children and youth are directed to consumption and performance, not to building relationships with adults—even their parents—whose lives might model faith, trust, and love.

Few children live close to grandparents or know any older adults intimately. Indeed, increasing numbers of children have few adults friends, few adult guarantors, few adult mentors, few adult heroes.[18] We might ponder for example, the effects of a generation whose heroes are drawn from the imaginations of cartoonists in comic books and on television. How futile are the feeble efforts in most congregations to inspire a future for youth through the random telling of stories and the chance relationships of adults in the congregation! The lack of significant adult relationships limits the power of the stories of faith we do tell children. They do not know the adults of the church well enough to discern the contemporary possibilities in those stories.

A similar statement is also appropriate for youth and adults who have just begun to enter into the meanings of the Christian story or whose journeys of faith call them to new understandings of those meanings for the questions or circumstances in which they now find themselves. If the relationships they develop do not bind them into the stories central to the identity and purpose of the church community, the creativity and vitality of the journeys of Moses, David, Esther, Mary, or Paul will have little meaning and power to them.

We must be cautious, however, as we assess the quality of the relationships in our congregations. Are they organized to value the differences in people, to honor the variety of gifts and graces that all bring? Are relationships ordered in patriarchal or hierarchical fashion, hindering the full expression of the variety of gifts and graces to be found in their memberships? I think of a congregation that had struggled hard to shift traditional male-female roles. It attempted to become aware of the racism in its organizational practices and interpersonal relationships. It was recognized for its hospitality to people from other religious faiths. But every Sunday morning near the front row during worship sat a teenager with Downs syndrome. He especially liked the music of worship. A few people took time to greet him each week. But it did not seem to dawn on anyone that he might have something to contribute besides his attendance, that he might like to be confirmed, or that he might have some gift to help build up the life of the congregation. The congregation's relational patterns did not include the possibility of mutuality between a person with a mental "disability" and other church members. This tendency to marginalize people—on the basis of age, mental or physical ability, race, language, ethnicity, gender, or sexual orientation radically diminishes the witness of congregations found in the vision of the church as the Body of Christ. That vision, which urges congregations to gather in *all* people from the highways and byways of life, contrasts vividly with the quest by many for congregational homogeneity.

Practicing a Communal Life-Style. Parker Palmer has suggested that an education for spirituality requires "practice."[19] The repetition of an action until its accomplishment achieves a high standard of performance is a critical component of learning. We recognize the importance of practice in sports and music. If we are parents of children we have watched them rehearse a musical scale, repeat attempts to throw the ball through a hoop, or decrease the time it takes to run from one place to another. Unfortunately little attention is given to the importance of practice in the church's education.

We do not read without practice. We cannot pray, sing hymns, or recite creeds if we have not practiced them. We do not recognize the pain in others if we have not practiced care for others. We do not know how to give leadership to a group if we have not practiced a multitude of relational and organizational skills. We do not know how to participate in transformational ministries of love and justice if we have not practiced the risks of being faithful in those places where people are hurting.

Practice is central to the habits, attitudes, and sensibilities that become second nature to people who live in a community seeking to incarnate the wisdom and compassion of Christ. Practice is critical to the kind of thinking that discerns the creativity and justice of God in the routines of daily life. Practice is essential to the vitality of congregational worship and practice increases the effectiveness of our service to others. Practice, indeed, should consume a significant amount of the educational attention of congregations. The need for practice is especially critical to the survival of communities of faith at a time in history when we are surrounded by many options for our commitments and we experience intense pressure to approach those commitments in much the same fashion as we choose a box of cereal from the grocery shelf. Lack of practice contributes to superficial faith and mission. It limits the freedom that can be achieved only through repeated practice. This is an insight most children discover at a fairly young age.

I grew up on an apple and pear farm. One of the ways I enlivened the tedious task of thinning excess fruit from the apple trees each June was to practice throwing apples we had removed from the trees at an increasingly smaller and more distant object. I still remember the exhilaration I experienced when I finally was able to knock another apple—less than one and a half inches in diameter—from a tree more than two rows away. Such is the foolishness of the young. But such is the wisdom of children. Practice leads to competency, even in the strange tasks children set for themselves.

A similar experience occurs for those who enter into the practice of daily prayer, Bible reading, serving the homeless, or thinking theologically about strategies to influence school board or city council decisions. The repetition of action in practice often seems like drudgery until we experience a breakthrough into a new level of competency. Then we find ourselves plumbing the depths of some new insight or probing expanded possibilities of serving others. We discover in the most practical way a sense of freedom, a sense of power to do that which lies before us.

Practice is not confined to our spiritual lives. Practice is central to the quality of a congregation's worship and mission. A children's choir director significantly heightened the experience of worship in one congregation over the years by having the children practice one hymn each week until they could sing at least one verse by memory. Over a year's time the children had developed quite a repertoire of the church's music that they could sing spontaneously. As these children (and those who followed them in that same practice) grew up and took their place as adult worshipers in that congregation, the liveliness of congregational singing increased. I will sometimes ask people in a workshop where they learned their favorite hymn. Often the answer will come back that it occurred in the opening exercises of Sunday school, or in a "sing along" activity during a youth ministry retreat or program. In each instance the frequent repetition of the hymn firmly helped to plant its tune and words in their memory.

Practice is similarly required for competence in ministries of service and justice. It is required for effective leadership of church and community groups. An occasional service project or weeklong work camp may be an inspiring experience, but they do not provide enough practice to create habits of service. A spontaneous response to support a cause or offer assistance does not lead to disciplined stewardship of money or time. For too long we have assumed that people are to practice something after they have learned about it in the classroom or study group. That may have worked in relatively homogeneous communities of faith with strong intergenerational ties undisturbed by a plethora of life-style, value, and commitment choices. But the faithfulness of congregational faith in most communities today requires practice to participate in each and every event designed to praise God and serve neighbor with all our hearts, minds, soul, and strength.

A major theme runs through this discussion of educational tasks for building communities of faith equipped to participate in acts of praise and service for the sake of the transformation of the world. We create communities of faith capable of praising God and serving neighbor most effectively in their preparation, engagement, and reflection on worship and mission. The continuity of the church requires the persistent re-creation of communities of faith across the generations. Two teaching tasks are central to this process. One is storytelling that occurs whenever and wherever people in congregations seek to reduce ignorance and nurture solidarity. The other is caregiving as a response to the claim of those stories on the imagination and actions of people in communities of faith.

Through storytelling we find models for our own care for others. Effective storytelling, however, also requires sensitive caregiving. The power of the story is enlivened by a gracious environment. Hostility limits any person's hearing. In the reciprocity of storytelling and caregiving, congregations may begin to live into and out of the primary events that give form and purpose to Christian life. Their interplay orders the continuity and renewal of congregational identity and vocation. Together they help equip congregations to praise God and serve neighbor.

EXERCISE IN CONGREGATIONAL ANALYSIS

Choose an event from the time line created in chapter 2. Identify where and how the four educational tasks identified in this chapter are found in the ways people are prepared to participate in that event and then reflect critically on its meanings for their lives.

4.

Making Meaning

I HAD A SIGNIFICANT RELIGIOUS EXPERIENCE when I was five or six. I had just gone to bed. My father was listening while I recited the Lord's Prayer. I got past the "hallowed" and the "trespasses," sailed through "the daily bread" to "the dimes in the kingdom." After pronouncing a firm "Amen," my father looked down at me, thought for a moment, and then said "There are no dimes in the kingdom." He then told me to say when I prayed, "For *thine* is the kingdom." As I now think about five-year-old sensibilities, "dimes in the kingdom" probably made more sense than "thine is the kingdom." Actually it probably made little difference which words I used at the time. The power of a prayer to a young child lies not in the words, but in the relationship of the child to the people who pray it. In this case the words were significant because they belonged to the vocabulary of my church and family. As we grow older, however, we have different expectations of the words we use. We increasingly want them to make sense on their own terms.

The quest for a "meaning-full" faith has become a distinctive challenge to contemporary church education.[1] Unfamiliar language, antiquated worldviews, and diverse life experiences increasingly limit the intelligibility of biblical, historical, and theological meanings for the average person. The problem of meaning is complicated by our growing awareness that truth and meaning are

socially constructed. They are related to the specific lin-
guistic nuances, symbolic systems, and social, political,
and economic situations of people. This means people
from two or more cultures may discern quite different
meanings from the same scripture text or religious experience. In similar fashion women and men, youth and
adults, poor and affluent may draw different meanings
from the same text.

Whenever a person teaches or preaches, the complex-
ity of the challenge to make sense of the texts central to
the life of the Christian faith community becomes evident. Perhaps the experience of one young pastor will
provide a common point of reference for our exploration of the need to revision the church's education so
that contemporary people are able to make sense of the
gospel for their lives.

THE WORDS OFFEND

This event occurred on the first Sunday of the month in
a small congregation in a community with an agricultural
and tourist economy. It was communion Sunday. Debbie
Stanley, the pastor, had studied child psychology and
developmental theory in college and seminary. These
studies had sensitized her to the importance of concrete
learning experiences for children. Seeing, touching, tast-
ing, and smelling, she discovered, heightened the potential for learning among children. She had discussed with
seminary classmates the possibility that tactile activities of
eating bread and drinking grape juice with family and
friends might well be one of the most tangible worship
experiences available to children. So she urged church
members to bring their children to the communion rail.

But Debbie Stanley had not reckoned with four-year-old
Gretchen. Words seemed to fascinate this small child. Dur-

ing her play she would situate herself to overhear adult conversations. She remembered what she heard. So as it turned
out, when Gretchen's mother asked if she would like to join
the family at the communion rail, Gretchen responded with
a loud stage whisper, "I am not going to drink anybody's
blood. I am going to the nursery." At which point she
walked out of the sanctuary and across the hall to the nursery. Everyone in that small church heard her.

The challenge for pastors and teachers seeking to
make ancient meanings relevant to the experience of
contemporary congregational worship becomes evident
in this story. How do we interpret symbolic language
rooted in the Jewish experience of exodus from bondage
in Egypt and the sacrificial heritage of Jewish temple
worship at the time of Jesus two thousand years ago to a
four-year-old who lives in the space age? The Jews no
longer perform animal sacrifices. Worldly-wise children
associate the word *sacrifice* primarily with the game of
baseball. How do we help children understand the relationship of this liturgical event to the acts of eating and
drinking? For most families, the event no longer has any
explicit connection to family rituals of eating or the family rehearsal of the stories of God's activity.

Nothing in Gretchen's immediate experience could
help her grasp the Gospel writers' meaning in those words.
And yet this challenge faces us every time we celebrate the
Eucharist and invite children to participate. The tempta-
tion is to simplify, sentimentalize, or trivialize the event and
its consequences to make it acceptable to their ears.

The challenge of interpreting texts written in a different age for people in different circumstances, however, is
not confined to the education of children. The issue is as
real for youth and adults. After this same service of worship a group of men stood outside the church discussing
Gretchen's outburst. An older leader of the congregation
confessed he agreed with her, but added, "I don't let

myself think about it." This lifelong church member could not make much more sense from that central event in the faith experience of the Christian community than could a four-year-old. The words, when heard literally by contemporary persons of any age, sound strange and barbaric.

This is not a new insight. In a similar discussion more than thirty years ago, J. Stanley Glen observed that modern persons regard the "ancient, supernatural perspective" of the Bible to be irrelevant. He shared with Hendrik Kraemer the sense that when many "lay members of the church" approached the Bible, they were overcome with a feeling of helplessness. They may have "a vague attitude of reverence for the Book," he noted, but they do not "know what to do with it." The problem suggested for Glen that the Bible (as well as the language of the creeds, many of the ancient prayers, and definitely much of the hymnody of the church) is unintelligible to a vast proportion of the people sitting in church pews. It may be experienced as beautiful and emotionally comforting but essentially "antiquated, archaic, unscientific," making it irrelevant, therefore, in corporation offices, factory assembly lines, or while negotiating city traffic.[2] For others it perpetuates social, economic, and cultural systems they find offensive. The words hinder our hearing good news.

Although a concern for the meaningfulness of the gospel caught the attention of numerous academic religious educators and a few curriculum writers and editors, especially during the 1960s and the 1980s, it has not penetrated what happens in many local churches. The consequences are increasingly evident.

REDUCTION OF RELIGIOUS THINKING

A Christian religious education that does not take seriously the problem of meaning runs the danger of reducing religious thinking to religious experience. The problem is evident in curriculum resource editorial policies driven by a marketing agenda. Most resources for youth and adults are written on a sixth grade reading level. Writers and editors then struggle with how to convey adult perspectives on issues through a child's vocabulary. This policy may make the church's educational resources "user friendly" for some, but it alienates others. It effectively limits the depth of discussion about significant matters of faith. It tends to perpetuate conformity rather than the transformation of the mind that Paul urged upon the Roman church.

The problem I am describing can be seen in the growing preference for musical slogans called choruses over the theological texts of hymns and spirituals in the music chosen for worship. It permeates the approach of many youth ministers who urge youth to develop a personal relationship with Jesus without a corresponding encounter with the Christ of history. In the resulting Jesusology, God is reduced to the warmth and intimacy of a personal protector and superfriend. It can be seen in the reduction of the gospel to "four laws" or "ten principles" as some do. It becomes evident in teacher recruitment when the expectations for their ministries center on creating pleasant experiences and warm relationships. Everything is kept easy and reassuring, evocative and busy.

The effect, Glen points out, is a kind of "lawlessness" that seeks "love without justice, repentance without restitution, freedom without discipline, gospel without law."[3] Personal experience takes over our quest to understand the truth of the gospel. Douglas John Hall calls this "thought-less faith," which he acknowledges is actually a contradiction in terms. Unfortunately its pervasiveness in our churches is but a "stage on the road to extinction" for Christianity and of civilization itself.[4] The situation is quite dangerous, because the survival of humanity requires meaning-full religious thought.

ISOLATION OF RELIGIOUS MEANINGS

Another example of the problem of meaning in the church's education may be found in the tendency to split religious meanings from the political, social, and economic spheres of our lives. Religious meanings are relegated to the private domains of home and faith community. Yale law professor, Stephen Carter, makes the point more force-fully. Religion, he writes, has actually been "banished" from public moral discourse by "political leaders, commentators, scholars, and voters" forcing "the religiously faithful to be other than themselves, to act . . . as though their faith does not matter to them" in the realm of work and politics. Robert Bellah and his colleagues, writing in *Habits of the Heart*, point out that the roots of the privatization of reli-gious faith and meaning run deep in United States history.

The official disestablishment of religion in the early nineteenth century contributed to the gradual shift from a public religious language to a "vague and generalized benevolence." Marginalized from the rest of the institu-tions of the community, religious communities and fami-lies continue to provide loving support for persons, but "no longer challenge the dominance of utilitarian values in the society at large." In a strange twist, Christian and Jewish congregations end up reinforcing the values of a hostile and fragmented world by "caring for its casual-ties" rather than by challenging its assumptions.[5]

This therapeutic function is perhaps most evident in church education for youth. Church leaders, appropri-ately concerned about the complex and dangerous world that permeates youth culture, prepare curriculum resources and plan educational "programs" designed primarily to help youth cope with the pressures they encounter. This therapeutic educational activity has its place, but it does not empower youth or the church at large to challenge the structures endangering their lives. It does not lead to any change in their situation. It does not equip them for a vocation of discipleship in a radically changing world. Instead it functions negatively by diminishing the influence of the gospel to the realm of personal choice and relationships. It conveys a gospel capable of helping people survive social pressures, but not one capable of confronting and overcoming the forces of evil that lie behind them. The isolation of religious meanings may be most real among young adults, however, who discover the religious values and ideas cherished in church are not welcomed in corporate discussions, even when dealing with issues of human worth, human dignity, or business ethics. To be religious in any public sense of the word requires the compartmentalization of faith meanings from their social and work worlds.

EXODUS FROM THE CHURCH

A third consequence of the lack of attention in church education to the problem of meaning may be seen in the exodus from the churches of many of the brightest and most capable of its youth and young adults. The decision to leave church, as Bellah has observed, no longer centers on the quest of youth to claim inherited religious meanings and practices for themselves. Many young people do not find in the church a source of meaning for their deepest and most pervasive questions.[6] Since congregational life increasingly functions in the private sphere of our lives, these young people, especially the college graduates among them, have little difficulty choosing to leave the church—many for good.

Recently I had the opportunity for an extended conversation with a high school senior. Her questions, concerns, and insights revealed a profound and thoughtful faith. She grew up in a congregation that valued its children and youth. It surrounded them with caring adults and committed teachers. It did not shy away from answering her questions. But she has begun to discover that the answers she received had value, not because they helped clarify her questions, but because she respected and trusted the people who gave them. Her world is now expanding. Her questions are more complex. The issues that trouble her are deeper. She no longer raises questions in her Sunday school class. The teacher provides simplistic answers that do not touch the heart of the problems she seeks to clarify. She has the growing sensation that a number of the people she has most trusted soon expect her to outgrow this phase in her life. Despite the leadership roles she fills in the church's youth ministry and the acceptance she experiences among adults, her general feeling is one of rejection.

Filling the void in her quest for meaning are two teachers at school who seem interested in her questions. They listen. They challenge her assumptions. They recommend extra reading. They suggested she volunteer to work with people who do not share the good fortune of her solidly middle-class home. Their conversations are providing her with a vocabulary that illuminates and deepens her search for meaning. That vocabulary is predominantly rooted in sociological, psychological, and literary concepts. Her faith vocabulary sounds increasingly irrelevant to her.

Her experience may well be compounded as she discovers the bias against religious meanings emerging from the personal and historical experience of women. She shares the cultural privileges of those in the U.S. and Canada whose ancestry can be traced to Northern Europe. But if her ancestry included historically marginalized cultures, her sense of alienation could well increase as she becomes conscious of the suppression of those interpretations emerging from her cultural traditions. If she follows the trends described in several studies of young adults in the church, this committed and thoughtful teenager will probably leave the church during college and never return. The church's education has not taken her quest for understanding seriously.[7]

EXERCISE IN CONGREGATIONAL ANALYSIS

Identify where in the life of your congregation children, youth, and adults have the opportunity to explore openly and freely their deepest questions about the meaning of religious faith for their personal lives, their families, their work, and their participation in political and social programs and institutions in your community. For example, I know a teacher of young adults who places a paper bag in the center of the classroom. Her students are invited to put questions they were afraid to ask into the bag anonymously.

Identify as well ways in which people are discouraged from asking questions of religious meaning in your congregation. A common example is the youth or adult class that spends all its time reading "the lesson" together and answering the teacher's questions about what the writer said.

EDUCATIONAL ELEMENTS IN MAKING MEANING

Why is the religious contribution to the human quest for meaning so problematic for many people today?

Webster's dictionary provides an initial clue in its definition of the word *meaning*. Something has meaning, according to Webster, if it has significance and purpose; if it is suggestive (*New Universal Unabridged Dictionary*). The action integral to the task of making meaning is a cognitive one. It involves actions of discerning, thinking, comprehending, and understanding. But we experience meaning affectively as coherence, discovery, and possibility. Meaning involves the interplay of cognitive and affective activity. In other words, our knowing and doing is intensified by our feelings and, conversely, our feelings are illuminated by our knowing. Their interdependence is a necessary condition for the commitment that gives impetus to our actions. Let's go back to Webster's definition for a moment. Something has significance if we "think" it is important. But its significance is enhanced if we also "feel" it is important. In a similar fashion, we may discern the purpose of something intellectually. But our relationship to that purpose has to do with its potential to motivate us—a willful and affective process.

Meaning involves more than the mutual exercise of thought and feeling. It engages us kinetically—the way we move our bodies, extend our arms and legs, contort our faces. One of the clues to the meaning of our teaching for students can be seen in their postures. Do their faces reveal the mental connections being made between ideas? Are they sitting up at attention? Are they squirming with excitement? These clues reveal the interactive dynamics of thinking, feeling, and physical movement in the processes of making meaning. When we analyze this interplay more closely we can begin to identify four actions in the processes of making meaning relevant to the educational effort of churches.

In the first place, as Ogden and Richards have observed, meaning at its most elementary level has to do with *the realization that words and things are somehow linked.*

Consciousness of that relationship is crucial to any effort we make to communicate with one another.[8] The common recognition that a certain configuration of legs, tail, hair, body shape, and the word *dog* go together is necessary for any conversation that might occur about dogs when none is present. But the affective content of that correspondence is most evident when a young child recognizes for the first time that the word *dog* connotes a specific kind of animal. That discovery of "naming" a specific kind of animal "dog" is an animating one, and unless the child has had a negative experience with dogs, is often punctuated with sounds of glee. Now that dogs are clearly a part of the child's world, she wants to pet every dog she sees.

The confirmation that the word *dog* identifies a certain kind of animal helps embed the child in a particular cultural expression of the human family. It distinguishes her from the French child who calls the same animal "chien." It creates a particular way of seeing and relating rooted in the possibilities and limits of the English language. She begins to order her experience of the world according to the rules governing the usage of that word in English. She begins to appropriate the subtleties of grammar and the nuances of values associated with the ways in which her family and community use that language. This process intensifies her identification with that community and its corporate memory. It embeds her in its ways of seeing and responding to the world around her.

The same process is integral to the life of the church as a community of faith. Gretchen heard her pastor invite people to "eat the body" and "drink the blood" of Jesus Christ. At the same time she had seen some of the women of the church pour grape juice into little cups and she had seen the loaf of bread people would be eating. Gretchen had no difficulty discerning the correspondence of "eating" bread and "drinking" grape juice. She liked both. Her mother often baked bread and her family grew grapes in their garden. These experiences expanded her conceptual and experiential awareness of the relationship of eating bread and drinking juice. But the correspondence between the concrete fact of the words *bread* and *juice* and the symbolic significance of body and blood escaped her comprehension. Indeed, her negative reaction creates an educational dilemma for her congregation. The negative correspondence she has made between the Eucharist and the literal meaning of eating body and drinking blood will have to be unlearned before she can move on to its symbolic meanings. Without careful attention to the negative content of that learning, she is a likely candidate for leaving church as she grows older.

If the members of the congregation want to intervene in a positive way to prevent such a loss, they might begin with the following questions.

When and where will Gretchen hear the stories of the Israelite flight from Egypt, the origins of Passover, the practices of sacrifice in Israelite worship, the feeding of the five thousand, the Last Supper, and Easter Sunday *often enough* to shape her imaginative understanding of the world around her?

When and where will she hear the people of that congregation share the stories of the "significance" of the Eucharist in their own lives?

Who will help her discover the social *and* symbolic "purposes" integral to the act of eating together in the context of thanksgiving and hospitality?

What will be the circumstances through which she might discover the responsibility growing out of the communal act of eating and drinking at the Lord's Table to the feeding of all God's children everywhere?

Where will she begin to hear about the justice implications in eating at the Lord's Table for the social, political, and economic order of all peoples in God's creation?

Similar questions should haunt our imaginations if we are to engage in an education that breaks open the symbolic meanings of this central event for Gretchen and for the children like her in our church communities.

The vitality of the life of any community depends upon the processes of nurturing ever deeper patterns of correspondence between word and fact in persons and groups. As in Gretchen's case, this effort often involves learning new patterns to replace outmoded or inadequate or wrong patterns. This process develops the shared meanings that make conversation possible. It validates community decisions and motivates community participation. It energizes worship and prompts congregational mission. But there is a not-so-hidden danger facing congregations seeking to help their members discover the correspondence between words originating in ancient events and relationships and the facts of contemporary experience.

The dynamics of the pluralism of contemporary life do not make our task easy. The plurality of perspectives on any interpretation of a biblical or theological text shatters many of our efforts for a shared meaning. Men and women will discern in the same text quite different meanings. The heritage of slavery and oppression influences African American readings of a text that are not visible to those whose ancestors dominated and oppressed them. Robert Allen Warner, a Native American theologian, points out that as the victims of conquest, Native Americans may not be able to read the story of Exodus with African American Christians as a journey of liberation.[9] Instead, through the experience of the conquered Canaanites their own relationship to the text might be more easily discerned. And with each cultural and socioeconomic group the complications for discerning shared meanings are increased.

The danger for the church, of course, is that meanings become intensely personal or situational. If they are to have any shared power some communal bond is necessary to facilitate the conversation in the church among diverse groups of people. That bond has historically tended to rely upon the dominance of one interpretation over another. The meanings of men have traditionally had more clout than those of women. The meanings associated with European American intellectual traditions have been given more credence than those from other cultures. And so we must confront the extent to which these examples of human pride and power influence the ways we view the meanings we make from our encounter with the gospel.

Sharon Welch, an ethicist, has suggested that in the diversity of perspectives in the human community, the only way we can build communities to embrace the mutuality of our quest for meaning is to engage those differences of correspondence between name and fact in acts of mutual critique. This would require an education sensitive to helping people hear inside the experience of the other, to discover sources to the meanings of others, and to identify together strengths and problems in the conclusions each party makes.[10]

For this reason we must probe a second characteristic of meaning crucial to our educational tasks. In more colloquial language, when something has meaning, we have *a sense of being at home* with the subject. The meanings are comfortable to us. Note the affective dimension inherent in the cognitive act of understanding something and note how this understanding of meaning requires that it be couched in terms of gender, culture, class, denomination, even age.

The dynamics of meaning run deeper than the correspondence of words and things. Sallie McFague has argued convincingly that in our positivist culture we too often take correspondence as equivalent to reality.[11] In other words, we do not move beyond the literal correspondence between word and thing to the symbolic content of that interaction. We share the problem of the man who did not want to struggle with making sense out of ancient sacramental words in the communion ritual.

Another common example may be seen in the difficulty some have with biblical descriptions of God as father because their own experience of fathers involves neglect, abuse, injustice. Rebecca Chopp provocatively argues that the dilemma for many women runs even deeper. Whenever we call God "Father" without a consciousness of the way that image helps to perpetuate patriarchal symbolic and social structures we reinforce the historic patterns of marginalizing women. Those structures limit the experience of God for people who have been oppressed or marginalized by them. They must look beyond the traditional assumptions that fatherhood could effectively symbolize God.[12]

For McFague the limits of correspondence are evident when the artist tries to duplicate or copy that which he or she is painting or when people use religious language as a copy of that which it represents.[13] This pattern is most evident in those who seek to hold onto language in literal forms, thereby limiting the activity of God to English translations of Greek and Hebrew words reflecting current usage in specific settings. The problem is compounded by the dynamic nature of language. The English of the King James, Jerusalem, and New Revised Standard Bibles reflect the quite different social, political, and theological contexts of their translators.

Michael Polanyi and Harry Prosch, whose writings on meaning have significantly influenced scholarly discussions on the subject, have another view. They suggest we live into the meanings we discern. We extend ourselves into what we find has coherence.[14] We take our place in the meaning. We find it dependable. We do not expect it to change suddenly. It creates an environment of trust that undergirds the freedom we feel as we allow ourselves to be pulled ever deeper into its possibilities. In this process we move beyond the literal correspondence between word and thing to encounter its symbolic potential. Perhaps we have now encountered meaning as "insight"—the capacity to see from the inside of something. We know more than the information on the surface of things. We do not have to rely on the descriptions of others. We participate in its possibilities.

This process is familiar to most of us. I still vividly remember when my encounter with the word *grace* moved beyond the literal associations of correspondence. I could use the word with ease. It was a common part of my church vocabulary. But for years its "meaning" had been limited to the concrete correspondence between the word and the fact of a prayer before meals, to the women who share the name Grace, and to the recognition that for some people "grace" had such "amazing" qualities they could only be described in song. Although I had been taught to identify certain happy or joyful events with grace and had heard others call such moments "filled with grace," the connections were not clear to me. The word belonged to others. It had social significance, but it did not have power to shape my imagination.

I was twenty-six years old and working in my office on some routine task, when with a flash of "insight," I "recognized" something of what grace meant, but this time, from inside the experience. Note the process of recognition. It involves the imagination. It moves beyond word to symbol. I could now begin to discern meanings beneath ancient and contemporary stories of "grace." That symbolic potential revealed in "new ways" the interdependence of God's acceptance and God's justice,

God's compassion and God's care. It provided a structure through which I could recall and relive with deepening appreciation prior moments of grace in my life. It called me, at the same time, to assume responsibility for embodying grace for others. I felt exhilarated, joyful, and connected in deeper ways to the community of grace.

This insight is critical for church education. Religious language does not move beyond the literal and the concrete until that point in time when people begin to feel at home with it enough to be engaged by its symbolic content. The challenge is compounded for us, because religious language and symbols are increasingly confined to the church and have little currency in our homes, work places, or public gatherings. And yet if we do not identify the public implications of religious meanings, the relevance of those meanings will not only be increasingly difficult to discern, but also increasingly irrelevant to daily decisions and relationships.

This brings me to a third characteristic of meaning. Meaning is integral to the human quest for *intellectual freedom.* One is not truly free to think until one has both a basic grasp of the correspondence of words and facts and enough familiarity with that interaction to begin to play with its possibilities.

The dynamics of being at home with a word, symbol, concept, metaphor, image, or method of knowing involves the freedom to explore its hidden potential and the demands those discoveries may make on our lives. This activity is doing theology. So, for example, in this effort, the Cross becomes more than a tree or two logs fashioned into an instrument for corporal punishment; it becomes a metaphor for the character of God. If we find ourselves claiming with the apostle Paul that through Christ we have been reconciled to God, then we begin to discover what it means to be ambassadors of

Christ to others (2 Cor. 5:20). In that role we see the Cross whenever and wherever we encounter suffering for the sake of another. Indeed, we take upon ourselves the possibilities of suffering for others. If we eat the bread and drink from the cup conscious of the demands of this act on our lives, we become agents of hospitality in a world full of strangers. We explore the limits of our responsiveness. We are reminded of the commonness and pervasiveness of God's activity in our midst. We are humbled by our finitude as we struggle to understand the religious meanings that motivate us. It is appropriate for us to ask whether or not the "back to the basics" movement in the schools or the insistence upon biblical inerrancy or doctrinal consistency by many church members may not be connected to the inability of people to see the correspondence between religious language and symbols and the events of their daily lives. When people today view an event of nature, their descriptions are at least quasi-scientific rather than religious in nature. We turn to psychotherapeutic rather than religious language to describe the problems in human relationships. We locate political and economic crises in the policies and actions of governments and industries and not in the failures of human responsiveness to the intentions of God's creative activity.

Should we be surprised, then, that mainstream and middle-class church people with a European American heritage lack the freedom within our churches to explore the nature of God out of the experience of feminist theologians or Latin American base communities? or to hear the word of God through Marxist judgments on the limits of capitalism? or to explore the possibilities of engaging in acts of praise and thanksgiving using the medium of rock music rather than the tavern music baptized for church use by Bach, Wesley, and others? Should we be surprised that the historic churches—black and white in the United States and Canada—have difficulty hearing good news through the religious experience of Christians whose ancestry encompasses Buddhist and Confucian traditions? These new ways of hearing and understanding will not make sense to us until we have the freedom to play with and explore the possibilities in the symbolic correspondence of word and experience in a variety of social and cultural contexts.

A fourth characteristic of meaning builds on the third. Meaning is central to *commitment*. Margaret Farley has observed that commitment involves "a willingness to do something." Robert Bellah and his colleagues make a similar assumption in their opening question to the preface of *Habits of the Heart*, "How ought we to live?" In both instances, commitment is the prelude to action.[15]

The impetus to commitment in meaning points to the necessary relationship between who we are as a people and how we live. It translates our values and ideals into actions that shape the character of interpersonal relationships, institutions, and political processes. It moves us beyond the obligations inherent in relationships based on loyalty or obedience. It binds people together in a common venture for the sake of the community's vision of the future of humanity.

Commitment is located in the capacity to make choices. The value of those choices, if they are free, depends on the extent to which we identify with their content and possibilities. The power of those choices depends upon the extent to which the associations of "word" and "fact" integral to the choice enliven our imagination, the extent to which we sense ourselves at home with their demands, and the intensity of our identification with their possibilities. These actions are all integral to the process of making meaning. In this regard meaning provides impetus to commitment and commitment intensifies the significance of meaning.

EXERCISE IN CONGREGATIONAL ANALYSIS

> Answer the following questions as a way to begin to identify how your congregation encourages its members to make religious meaning for their lives. After completing the questions, review the four points in the section above about the nature of meaning, and then identify strengths and problems you see in your congregation's education for making meaning religiously. Keep a copy of this information for use with "A Guide to Revisioning Local Church Education."

CONTEXTS FOR MAKING MEANING

1. What resources for biblical interpretation would your high school seniors use when they want to understand the meaning of a passage or story?

2. What similarities and differences could they identify between the worldviews, cultural assumptions, and religious values in the writings of Paul (or any other part of scripture) and our own time?

3. When and where do they have the opportunity to explore how the words and stories written for one place and time might become useful to people in our time?

4. When and where do they have the opportunity to explore implications for their lives from the variety of interpretations they discover can be drawn from a biblical passage or a theological text?

5. What leadership skills do they possess for leading people of all ages in prayer, worship, public reading of the

Bible, sharing their faith, planning an event or program, delegating responsibilities, working cooperatively, critiquing ideas and plans theologically and ethically, and so on? Where do they receive the opportunities to be trained for these roles?

6. What criteria would your high school seniors use from their Christian education experience to choose a college, a career, a partner in life?

7. What doctrines, teachings, stories would your high school graduates be most likely to use to evaluate the worth and integrity of public policies and candidates for public office?

A DISCIPLE COMMUNITY

When congregations facilitate the quest for meaning, they engage in theological education. This conviction has led several prominent Christian educators to suggest that congregations model their education after the theological school. They emphasize the intellectual processes for making meaning and stress a sequential curriculum and a hierarchical relationship between teachers and students. This approach misses the distinctive structures for making meaning integral to congregational reflection in its worship and mission.

Douglas John Hall, a Canadian theologian deeply concerned about the relevance of Christian belief to contemporary living, has made another suggestion. He urges us to look on the church as a *disciple community*—a community engaged in and committed to theological self-reflection. Christian meanings emerge from the reflection of the church *on* the "subject matter of the Christian faith" *with* those "who struggle with this subject matter and live in the sphere of its influence."[16] From this perspective every congregation, if it seeks to be faithful, engages in disciplined meaning making. Its method emerges from the experience of the disciples originally gathered around Jesus seeking to understand the confusing and awesome things happening to them. It continues to develop in the struggles of the early church to be faithful after the death of the apostles. It continues down through the ages to the specific communal responsiveness of contemporary local congregations to the grace-full activity of God in Jesus Christ.

A story from another congregation may illustrate my point. Northside Church had been organized in a local elementary school in the midst of a new suburban subdivision. The young pastor energetically visited families moving into the neighborhood. He soon acquired a reputation in the community as a strong prophetic preacher and advocate for social justice. Many people attracted to the congregation were young adults who had been turned off by traditional church life and tedious church education. Although the provocative preaching of the pastor excited them, they could not be persuaded to participate in adult education unless the pastor was teaching.

Over the years the congregation increasingly struggled to find ways to order its worship life so that it would be "meaningful" to a membership lacking basic knowledge about the beliefs and history of the church. Many in the congregation hungered for a deeper faith. Somewhere along the way two decisions distinctively reshaped the education of the congregation. The first was to create committees to help plan the liturgies for the various seasons of the church year. Often several committees would be established to deal with a range of tasks including choosing the theme for the season, decorating the worship space, planning the music, interpreting the season to the congregation, relating mission emphases, and planning liturgies and congregational events.

The second decision followed, and these committees

became a primary center for the discussion of theological and liturgical texts and their meaning for the people of Northside Church. People discovered they could not carry out their responsibilities without first understanding the biblical and theological themes integral to the season. The committees would often begin their work months in advance so as to provide enough time for their knowledge of the season to be adequate to clarify the relevance of the season to the congregation. In its own way the education the members of these committees received was as orderly and systematic as could be found in any class using traditional church school curriculum. The difference was the practical usefulness of their study in the life of the congregation. Their discussions spilled over into church business meetings, the church hallways, fellowship suppers, and in the supermarket when people happened to meet.

Northside illustrates several characteristics of a disciple community. First, by focusing its energies on seasonal events of congregational life (in this case, weekly worship), it emphasized *congregational mutuality in its education*. Children learned hymns and songs in Sunday school for worship. Many people discussed the meaning of designated biblical texts in planning meetings, choir rehearsals, and in some Christian education classes. People practiced new parts of the liturgy prior to the event. And the services were interpreted in newsletters and a variety of congregational gatherings.

Second, Northside promoted *the partnership of clergy and laity* in theological reflection. Clergy often provided an introduction to the theological heritage and significance of a season. Groups spent more time in research and study than in listening to the theological interpretations of experts. The educational role of clergy shifted consequently from being transmitters of specific views on biblical and theological themes to being resource persons and consultants to the educational venture.

Third, *the local congregation became a primary context for theological reflection.* Northside reclaimed its partnership in the theological enterprise with theologians, pastors, and curriculum writers. This meant that their engagement with the gospel in any church season had more opportunity to be relevant to the specific issues and circumstances of the local community. Their thinking about faith revealed the dialogical encounter between the tradition of faith received and the efforts to live faithfully in a given context. When this theological reflection does not occur in the congregation, laity are removed from the dialogue. They become observers and recipients rather than actors and contributors.

Fourth, *theological meanings* at Northside emerged from the *negotiations among a variety of perspectives* (gender, generational, ideological, socioeconomic, and cultural) held by church members and those with whom they associated regularly during the week. Even when selecting hymns for worship, people discovered that assumptions about familiarity, taste, theological content, and relevance to gender and cultural sensitivity had to be identified and explored before a decision could be made.

Fifth, for the people of Northside meaning emerged from their *struggle against irrelevance.* Their conversations persistently revealed the "alienation of spirit"[17] caused by texts and practices that people did not understand, appreciate, or trust. An overriding question in their discussions had to do with whether or not something they did would enable the people of the congregation to hear good news adequately for a response in their daily lives.

Sixth, in the shared commitment to "meaningful" worship, the members of Northside engaged in *disciplined reflection for a better comprehension of the liturgical events they were planning and the implications of those events for their lives.* The energy revealed in the dedication of Northside members to their work locates the sources to this discipline in their quest to understand rather than in obedience to rules or dogma. Their commitment is evident in the several months of preparation it took to be ready for the celebration of each liturgical season. Perhaps that dedication developed because church members discovered possibilities rather than limits in the messages of the event(s) that empowered rather than restricted relationships.[18]

These six steps also marked the educational approach of Northside Church to its major missional efforts. When the city's schools were placed under a court order to desegregate, a congregational task force provided a forum for biblical and theological study of reconciliation. On another occasion, the congregation began the study of the role of faith communities in promoting good health. This project led to the establishment of a wellness clinic in the church building. In each instance, a mutual quest to understand the issues involved in the context of their faith traditions gathered the wider circles of the congregation's membership into a process of reflection and decision making as a basis for action in the community.

EXERCISE IN CONGREGATIONAL ANALYSIS

Review the six characteristics of a Disciple Community. Which does your congregation take most and least seriously? Give examples. Record and keep this information for use with "A Guide to Revisioning Local Church Education."

TEACHING FOR MEANING

Teachers, rather than programs and instructional agencies, give shape to event-full education. The quest for meaning originates as gaps in our knowledge and skill become evident to us. It occurs whenever our words are not adequate to the task of naming our experience; when the symbols we use cannot convey the intent of our words or actions; when in the course of our inquiry or work we cannot think of alternative perspectives or approaches; and when our commitments seem inadequate to the challenges before us. Teachers for meaning step into these gaps to engage us in a process to bridge, mediate, or appreciate the gap. Teachers who facilitate our quest for meaning engage in several tasks.

1. Teachers invite students into activities of interpretation to explore the ancient and unfamiliar worlds that lie behind a passage of scripture, story, liturgical, or missional act. They help students begin to discover meanings for a scripture passage, for example, as it might have been understood by the author, the first people who heard it, or by people who have heard that same text in a different situation and through quite different cultural perspectives. As Robert McAfee Brown has pointed out, as these meanings become increasingly open to us, we make decisions about their importance to us. Some become normative for our lives. We choose to live out of their content. As we become increasingly aware of the content of the meanings in those events, they may contribute to the transformation of our lives.[19]

2. Teachers invite students into activities of interpretation to help them become conscious of their own embeddedness in the cultural ethos of their families, churches, ethnic heritage, and nation. In this process students begin to see themselves in their social and religious context with the same clarity that others can. Eventually they may begin to see themselves from the perspective of the biblical and theological texts that they are also exploring. This process is evident when some people discover their experience reflected in a reading of the Exodus, the

Exile, or the struggles of the church in Corinth. It is also evident when some middle-class churchgoers encounter in a direct way the judgment of Jesus regarding their disregard of the poor in their communities. In such discoveries they confront the "meaning bias" they bring to their reading of scripture or to their participation in a liturgical or missional act. They begin to see themselves from the vantage point of the text rather than from their own experience.

3. Teachers invite students into activities of interpretation to help them develop skills to make sense of the gaps they discover between their own views and those found in biblical and other ancient texts and in the institutional and liturgical traditions they encounter. The teacher helps them become aware of the ideological bias in the skills they are using—does it promote patriarchal, or elitist, or American U.S. assumptions? The teacher helps them make judgments about the appropriateness of any methodology of interpretation for the questions or problems they seek to resolve.

4. Teachers as interpreters help students discover both the connectedness and the irreconcilable differences of the total human experience vertically (across the generations) and horizontally (across the cultures and communities of the world). Teachers in the quest for meaning then encourage students to risk an interpretive act—to attempt to construct a statement or action that accounts for both the mutuality and the diversity they encounter from the multiple voices they hear from the text and the setting out of which one reads it. This is an audacious act. It can separate a person from the community. It can effect reconciliation. It can evoke solidarity. It can lead to judgment. The quest for meaning, in other words, is both urgently sought and feared.

5. For that reason teachers who invite students into acts of making meaning may find themselves the object

EXERCISE IN CONGREGATIONAL ANALYSIS

Where does interpretive teaching consistently take place in your congregation?

Who are the people who engage others in activities to make meaning from the encounter with scripture and the church's traditions with their daily lives?

What strengths and problems do you see in your congregation's efforts to help people make religious meaning?

Make lists of your answers to these questions for later use.

of a student's quest for a mentor. Mentors model the quest for meaning for students. They do not give answers. They create environments of grace or safe places where students may test their interpretive constructions for their faithfulness to the intentions of the gospel and for their relevance to the place and circumstances of their lives.

Interpretive teachers are usually assigned to classes. That can be an effective context for teaching if transmissive teaching patterns are not permitted to dominate the order of study. Interpretive teaching may actually be most relevant to a congregation when it occurs at the critical points where people's questions, issues, and problems of meaning are most evident. Do people know enough about the context of the scripture lessons that frame the sermon to hear more than its words? If not, that may say something about the need to prepare people to hear through classes prior to worship, the weekly newsletter, or during a weeknight Bible study. Do people bring a larger theological and ethical grasp of the situations surrounding the various administrative decisions regarding mission, budget, building, or community service? If not, that may say something about how time is spent in committee meetings to ensure enough insight from the traditions of faith to illumine decisions for ministry. Teaching for meaning, in other words, may occur in regularly scheduled classes, during pastoral calls, or in the midst of administrative meetings. Some moments for teaching for meaning are regularly scheduled. Others must be seized whenever gaps in knowledge and experience hinder the people of faith as they seek to become a Disciple Community.

5.

Nurturing Hope

A PERVASIVE DESPAIR

Like the fog creeping through the streets and shrouding the buildings of San Francisco, a deep and pervading sense of despair penetrates the hearts and minds of growing numbers of people in the United States and Canada. It has caught the attention of the media. A recent article announced that the "Future looks bleak to anxious, pessimistic adolescents." Peter Benson, whose research has included responses from more than one hundred thousand teenagers, is quoted as seeing a new kind of pessimism among them. Youth report being "disconnected from social institutions and support systems." They have "a sense of powerlessness to make a difference." A *Washington Post* poll of twelve- to seventeen-year-olds prior to the 1992 election discovered that 60 percent believed "America's best years are over." This kind of pessimism may help explain the fourfold increase in the number of teenagers who have contemplated suicide, and the growing tendency—even among church youth—to engage in activities that put their lives at risk.[1]

The lack of hope for the future is not limited to the experience of teenagers. Apathy and despair, anger and cynicism, fickle loyalties and tentative commitments are prominent themes in contemporary films, literature, and television shows. It lies behind the fears many people talked about during the 1992 presidential election campaign regarding a breakdown in the social order and a collapse of law and order in the nation.

The tentativeness in our hoping reaches into the heart of congregational life. Another story may help illumine this challenge to future church education. This story is especially relevant to our discussion, because it centers on a very active and committed woman approaching retirement in her professional life. I first met Anne when I began teaching an adult Sunday school class. She had been an active member of the church and Sunday school throughout her life. She was the kind of student a teacher loves. She not only read her Sunday school lesson prior to Sunday morning, but she also sought out additional educational opportunities to extend and deepen her knowledge of the faith.

One Sunday, during a discussion on prayer, she asked, "What can one pray for when a loved one is in crisis?" Her words sounded like a question on the methodology of intercessory prayer. But this was not the usual kind of question she would ask. So I encouraged her to help us understand her question. A summary of the issues she then raised included several profound concerns.

As a "modern" woman, she no longer had any idea "where" God is. As an adherent of a scientific point of view, she could no longer conceive of a God who would interrupt the laws of nature so that someone she loved might avoid their consequences. As a woman with a keen sense of justice she could no longer imagine a God who would answer her prayer and, at the same time, ignore the prayers of someone else in crisis. Although she still believed that God must be able to make a difference, she could no longer describe what that difference might be with any confidence. She no longer possessed either the theological language or categories to express satisfactorily a personal and modern faith in God.

Her questions disturbed her. She assumed that at her age she should be able to draw upon the experiences of her journey of faith for insights into her present situation—a view congruent with Erik Erikson's understanding of the developmental task of generativity. But she faced instead the realization that the culmination of her faith journey might lie not in the concreteness of her relationship to God, but in her faith in the possibility of that relationship.

She reminded me of the words of the Digger Indian chief I quoted in the Introduction. Her words were filled with a longing for the clarity and confidence of the faith she had enjoyed as a younger woman. They conveyed a sense of resignation over her diminished sense of influence in an increasingly complex and terrorized world. And yet, unlike the Digger chief, she concluded our discussion with a commitment to the future. She continued to pray, to hold onto the idea that faithfulness can make a difference. This affirmation is not likely to create a groundswell of enthusiasm for church education or to attract significant numbers of new members into our churches. And yet Anne's confrontation with the possibility that her prayers might not make any difference to those for whom she prayed may provide a clue to the desperate disillusionment creeping into the questions of the most active youth and adults in our educational ministries.

EXERCISE IN CONGREGATIONAL ANALYSIS

List perceptions you had of the world when you were ten or eleven years old. What is the world like for today's ten-year-old? Make another list with these thoughts. Mark the most significant differences between these two lists. Which things on your contemporary list do you experience as promise and which as threat to the future of today's children? Keep your answers for use later.

LOSS OF HOPE

We cannot adequately discuss what church education should be doing until we acknowledge the extent of the loss of hope in the people of our communities and the members of our churches. The loss of hope can be explicit and direct. We encounter it in the fear of dying among many people in nursing homes. We hear it in the words of many older adults who choose to live in housing or communities established only for adults. We see it in congregations that discourage the participation of children in worship or that do not include children in direct mission activities. We see it in the resistance of people to governmental policies and programs designed to ensure the nutritional and educational future of children.

It lies behind the high rate of mental illness and the soaring number of suicide attempts among adolescents. It contributes to the self-destructive behavior that begins for many in elementary school and peaks among teenagers and young adults—especially among young men. It undercuts the productivity of men and women who fear for the future of their jobs. It is seen in the apathy of the homeless and jobless. These symptoms, however, point to a deeper fear—the loss of a viable future.

The sources of this deeper fear reside for the most part just beyond our consciousness. They intrude into our dreams. They subvert moments of joy and turn achievements into shallow accomplishments. I see at least three sources of this gnawing fear that the future is hopeless. The weight of their claims on the human spirit is all the more serious because little attention has been paid to them.

LIVING AT THE EDGE OF HISTORY

In *Theology for a Nuclear Age*, Gordon Kaufman, a contemporary theologian seeking to understand the impact of the modern world on the way we believe, reminds us that we face the end of history in a way unimaginable to our ancestors. Deeply rooted themes in the Jewish and Christian apocalyptic literature about God's intervention in human history seem strangely out of place when considering the consequences of nuclear destruction or environmental pollution. The holocaust haunts our imaginations with an increasing number of forms: the violence of war, the pollution of earth's life sustaining resources; the insatiable demands of a burgeoning population; pernicious and fatal diseases resisting treatment; and the deterioration of the ozone layer. The fear that lies beneath our conversations has in recent years been symbolized by Iraq, Somalia, and Bosnia, and by the beating of Rodney King and the assault on a truck driver who happened into a hostile intersection in Los Angeles. That fear is further imprinted on our senses by the irrational murders of colleagues by disgruntled workers, the chemical pollution of farmland, and the discovery of arsenals of biological and chemical weapons in several nations that are driven by the grandiose dreams of arrogant demagogues. These forms of destruction have little to do with a plan of salvation to be found in the Bible or church tradition. Their effect is destruction, not re-creation, and their outcome forebodes the extinction and not the salvation of human life. For the first time in human history we ponder not just our own fates but that of the world itself.

The capacity to obliterate the human race, Kaufman reminds us, is so novel and strange, so difficult to grasp, "so abstract, so empty of meaning, that we can scarcely grasp what we are talking about." Yet it haunts our corporate imaginations, creeps into the dreams of our children, and creates fear in grandparents for the future of their grandchildren. For the first time in history, we possess the destructive capability to "bring us up against the ultimate limits of our human existence"—limits beyond which we cannot envision a safe and viable future for ourselves or our children.[2]

How do we make sense out of living at the edge of history? In the past our religious narratives located possibilities in the actions of God. We search through the wisdom of this heritage for clues to guide our efforts to make sense out of these threats to the future of humanity. But we will not find any visions of messianic banquets or promises of peaceful kingdoms filled with gentle lions and brave lambs that lie beyond the annihilation of the human race. Instead increasing numbers of peoples find themselves confronting the terrifying possibility that in this situation the trust of their ancestors in the sovereignty of God may be irrelevant.[3]

What does it mean to live at the edge of God's history with the people of earth? The silence for many (especially the young) is awesome. The weight of that oppressive silence intrudes upon our efforts to make sense out of our lives. It disrupts the order of our thoughts and creates a sense of futility for the efforts of many to see purpose in their decisions and actions. It calls for a new kind of educating.

AT THE EDGE OF OUR HUMANITY

Another fracture in the church's education contributing to a loss of hope may be traced to the challenges we experience about what it means to be human. The revolution in genetic research and medical technology, for example, calls into question many of our deepest assumptions about what it means to be human in God's image, the subject and agent of God's ongoing creativity. During the past fifty years we have learned how to control the reproduction of life. We persistently seek ways to eliminate genetic disorders that intrude on qualities of life we value. We can now determine, with some margin for error, the sex of our children. We substitute organs from one body to another almost as freely as we remove an appendix. We create artificial organs and limbs that may eventually last longer and work more efficiently than our natural ones. Perhaps most significantly, scientists gradually are revealing the secrets involved in the creation of life itself.

These discoveries fill me with awe. They reveal my phenomenal ignorance of the vastness of the mystery of the universe. I am both humbled and excited by the promises in these discoveries for the betterment of the human experience. Reports of the scientists' work enliven my imagination regarding the intricacies of the created order as well as the phenomenal capacity of humanity to unlock the mysteries of that order.

As I listen carefully to the discussions I have had in local church education settings, however, I am confronted with the fact that with every major genetic and medical discovery, old and familiar structures regarding our understanding of our relationship to God are altered. One example: a pastoral call in the hospital confronts us with the tension between traditional religious symbols of healing and the new technologies that brush aside their relevancy. New questions emerge from the recesses of our consciousness. We find ourselves sharing Anne's dilemma about what and how to pray.

Where is the power of prayer if, in fact, our petitions do not affect any change? What does it mean to thank God for the capacity to reconcile and restore when the restoration we experience is based on chemical therapy or filled with plastic? What does it mean to die and to live again in God's eternal grace when we no longer can agree when death occurs, much less what death signifies? What does it mean when researchers announce a new breakthrough in the quest to control disease and the evening news describes yet another, even more virulent and extremely dangerous disease?

As we leave the hospital room, those questions prompt others equally as haunting. Some highlight our inability to sort out the ethical consequences of the ingenuity in human creativity. What is the value of existence when we permit both hundreds of thousands of fetuses to be aborted and hundreds of thousands of other babies to die through starvation, war, or abuse each year? What is the meaning and value of a life in the competition for organs? What is the meaning and value of a life sustained by costly life preserving techniques while increasing numbers of children are deprived of basic medical and dietary needs? In our fascination with preserving the lives of a few, have we lost sight of our responsibilities for the continuity and renewal of the human race itself?

Ultimately our questions have to do with what it means to be human. Although suggestive, the old answers do not fit many of our new questions. The silence from theologians and the pulpit in exploring these questions, however, is also significant. They seem to have retreated from many of the toughest questions about what it means to be human for our own time. The people in our congregations, however, must answer them in the daily course of family responsibilities. In that effort they may have congregational support. They may be sustained by the love of the people of the church. But rarely does their church education provide any clear guidance from the study of the church's traditions for the personal and global decisions they must make regarding life and death.

AT THE EDGE OF PREDICTABILITY

The collapse of structures that fill life with hope may be traced to at least one other source. Physical scientists continue to probe our knowledge of the universe into ever more sophisticated and refined realms. Their discoveries reveal the intricacies of creation to be greater than our ancestors had imagined in their wildest fantasies. Their discoveries again fill us with wonder and awe.

Many scientists now say that the order and harmony we perceived in nature through the categories of ancient and classical science may actually be more illusion than fact. In a provocative "meditation on the relationship of humanity to the universe," physics Nobel prizewinner Ilya Prigogine and his colleague Isabelle Stengers explore the changing conceptual structures guiding scientific study. Of primary interest to them is the shift in the attention of scientists from the unchanging and predictable character of substance to the multiple and spontaneous dynamics of time.[4]

One illustration may clarify the radical effects of their work on the assumptions we make about the world around us. We assume an action leads to a given reaction. When a softball hits a bat, we "know" it will fly away from the batter. Where it goes depends on the spin of the ball, the place the ball hit the bat, and the power of the swing. We assume that if we know this information we can predict where a ball might land. This assumption grows out of our conviction that the principles of cause and effect are integral to the nature of reality.

Many scientists have come to another conclusion. They view the actions of cause and effect in statistical rather than metaphysical terms. This means they can verify the consequences of a bat hitting a ball in an experiment, but they no longer can verify that reality itself is based upon the consequences of a principle of causality or that all things might even be caused. We may encounter the consequences of this new idea on our faith statements when we attempt to interpret the familiar text from the book of Genesis, "In the *beginning* God created. . . ." We have traditionally viewed that phrase as the context for a first act setting in motion other actions in the order of creation. This notion has been reinforced for us by mechanistic notions of causality inherited from the Enlightenment thinkers of the eighteenth century.

Some scientists now insist that randomness or happenstance is as much a part of reality as the orderliness we see in the relationship of cause and effect. That insight is most familiarly expressed in Einstein's theory of relativity, but we experience its possibilities whenever something intrudes upon our routines and nothing then seems to go right for us. We use a variety of words and phrases to describe situations in our lives that we cannot fully understand. We say "we had a bad day." We complain that "nothing I do seems to be going right." Or we may exclaim that "things are chaotic" or that "my life is out of control." What we mean, these scientists contend, is that we no longer can predict what will happen next. For a time, at least, the options overwhelm or elude us.

This shift in scientific thinking has barely penetrated the language or thinking of the church. Although familiar to the nuclear engineers I have taught, I can barely grasp either its content or implications. In our ignorance we perpetuate language and theological concepts that hold on to and extend pre-Copernican views of the natural order and of the relationship of the sacred and the mundane into our religious discourse. People still talk as if God were directionally "up" somewhere, for example. We continue to organize congregations on social principles drawn from mechanistic worldviews identified with the eighteenth-century Enlightenment. We still act as if teachers telling students what they should know will produce student learning. We still believe we can control our schedules and manage our time.

We continue to assume we should be able to envision

our future from assumptions about the orderliness of creation we have inherited from the past. But daily experience persistently undermines those expectations. We find ourselves then asking for what can we hope when chaos and confusion seem to dominate our consciousness. It certainly cannot be found in a church education that promotes some form of biblical literalism with its sense of absolutism. It certainly cannot be found in the transmission of theological dogmas couched in words and concepts drawn from an earlier view of the order and structure of reality. It certainly cannot be sustained over time by edicts from church authorities about what should and should not be taught. The sense of hope in these approaches to the content of faith direct our attention to the past and not to the future from which God beckons us.

Despite our efforts to hold on to sources of hope valued by our faith ancestors, we confront our own lack of hope in fractious church and civic committee meetings, in the fatigue we feel when facing a new challenge or task. We discover it in our confusion about the object of our commitments. We recognize it whenever our words sound hollow and our efforts enervate rather than energize us. Ultimately the loss of hope is revealed in our lack of vocational clarity as individuals and as congregations. The vision that once inspired us; the call that once motivated us; the traditions that used to feed and nurture us end up sounding like clanging gongs and cymbals. Our sense of emptiness makes us easy prey for quick fix consultants making large profits from troubled churches, while the spiritual emptiness of many in our congregations leads them to try the latest fads to improve self-esteem, experience the power of holiness, or elicit some sense of intimacy with others. We see it in the frantic rush to mount ever more attractive programs, to find an even more stimulating teacher or better curriculum, to try any new videotape that might be acceptable, to adopt the latest technological innovations to intensify the experience of worship and heighten our sense of something spiritual.

Part of the responsibility for the diminishment of hope must be traced to flaws in the educational ministries of our congregations. Church education no longer provides an adequate structure for communicating hope. More than thirty years ago many of us sang enthusiastically with Bob Dylan that the times were "a-changing." We looked toward a new moral order growing out of the powerful images of peace and love in our faith traditions. We caught Martin Luther King Jr.'s dream for a new America, a new world. We envisioned a new age beyond racial oppression, military aggression, and technological tyranny built on the visions of the prophets. In the meantime, we did not recognize the forces at work in our midst, indeed forces to which we also contributed, that now create the conditions for new visions of hope to dispel our despair. So what does it mean to revision church education in the face of the contemporary loss of hope?

EXERCISE IN CONGREGATIONAL ANALYSIS

Identify where you see a loss of hope most vividly in your congregation. To what extent can you trace it to
• a loss of a sense of possibility in the future?
• changing assumptions about what it means to be human?
• A sense that the world is overwhelmingly chaotic and confusing?
What other forces do you find at work debilitating the vitality of your congregation's worship and mission? Record and keep this information for use with "A Guide to Revisioning Local Church Education."

EDUCATION FOR HOPE

We continue to *organize our educational ministries as if present experience extends the experience of the past, as if old images are adequate for the contemporary quest for hope.* This assumption is not adequate; indeed, it has never been adequate to the educational challenge of the church in any age. Our task of understanding the gospel is different from the task Jesus had in awakening the disciples to the meaning of his presence in their midst. It is different from the task Paul had in those years of study between his encounter on the road to Damascus and the beginning of his missionary journeys. It is different from the task facing Thomas Aquinas as he tried to clarify Christian beliefs in light of the concepts of Greek philosophy during the Middle Ages. It is different from the task facing our colonial ancestors as they tried to understand the blessing and responsibility of establishing and securing a new nation.

We live not only after Paul, Aquinas, Luther, Wesley, Copernicus, Galileo, Newton, and Darwin. We also live after Einstein and the theory of relativity and after Prigogine and Stengers' articulation of a theory of chaos. Again our dilemma has two edges. Many in our churches are like the farmer who steadfastly proclaims loyalty to the biblical accounts of creation as literally true on Sunday morning and follows the principles of evolution in the selection of farming practices the rest of the week. Many are like the teenagers who seek out places to worship where the words of liturgy and sermon do not limit the activity of God to specific Christian traditions. Many are like the biologist, nurse, art teacher, corporate executive, lawyer, many women and many members of racial and cultural minority groups who no longer attend church because they do not hear there a word of hope that illumines their ethical and vocational decisions.

If the church is to have a vision that infuses our lives with hope for the future and that mobilizes our energies for faithful responding to the possibilities for humanity in that vision, we need a context where people might encounter the creative and redemptive activity of God at work, where the exploration of new images for God's activity is affirmed, and where the exercise of the imagination is deliberately and intentionally nurtured. What does that context look like?

Those same studies we quoted earlier describing the increasing cynicism among teenagers provide a clue. Researchers wanted to find out what was going on in the lives of the youth who were not depressed, pessimistic, or cynical. They found two constant themes in the responses of these youth. They were involved in continuing acts of service to others and they had significant adult friends. The religious significance of these two themes should not be hard to locate. A major source of hope is to be found in our participation in God's vocation in the human experience. Perhaps a story from another congregation will illustrate a way to begin to talk about an education that nurtures hope.

WE'RE THE ONLY ONES

Community Church is located on the edge of a large city in the southeastern part of the country. During the 1960s and early 1970s, growing numbers of people from the city built new homes and neighborhoods around this small country church.[5] The church welcomed them and the membership increased. Plans were made to build a new sanctuary. Then the neighborhood changed.

This community had been predominantly white. By the mid-seventies most new residents were black. Church membership declined as families with children and youth moved away. All the problems of a changing community altered the life in this quiet community. Violence in the schools, latch key children running around the neighborhoods, fear and tension between old-timers and newcomers threatened a sense of community well-being. In 1980 this congregation received a new pastor—a woman who accepted the position after several men had turned it down.

She invited children from some of the new families in the neighborhood to Sunday school and a few came. Eventually some of their parents began coming. She listened to people talk about their anxieties and fears. She shared her concerns for the children of working parents who lacked supervision after school. About the time when most congregations in transition become discouraged and turn in on themselves, these conversations culminated in a decision by the remaining members "to stabilize the neighborhood," in part, because they could not see anyone else who could or would do it. That decision radically altered this congregation's future.

The signs of that change can be seen in many places. On a nice day church members—white and black—stand around after worship on the church lawn engaged in conversation for thirty or more minutes. Every meeting and church activity begins and ends with similarly extended conversation. At first I thought this activity was primarily a time for socializing. Later I discovered that during these conversations people often shared ideas and explored issues affecting their community. Much of that discussion centers around the schools in which parents and pastor are deeply involved to support their children and to create an educational environment conducive to quality education for all children and youth.

When one walks into the recently renovated sanctuary, a stained glass window depicting Jesus surrounded by children with dark and light skin hues catches one's eye. Then one begins to notice children seemingly everywhere. They are present and actively involved in great numbers in worship and most gatherings of the church—including those business meetings when the church votes on crucial issues. They are hugged and disciplined by black and white adults in spontaneous acts of affection and concern. "We are family"—one African American man explained to us. The power of that statement in a multiracial congregation became evident when he concluded that we could tell this was true "because we eat in each other's homes all the time." The table, in other words, whether it be in their homes for a congregational dinner, or in the sanctuary for the Eucharist, symbolized their solidarity as a community of faith.

A gym dwarfs the sanctuary and educational buildings. It was built by church members because the community needed a place where the church's integrated basketball team could play without being subjected to racial slurs. It is now the center of community life. Basketball and volleyball teams from all over the region play in that gym, bringing together people with African, Asian, European, and Hispanic heritages. People gather in that place to discuss community issues and to vote. A weekday after school program and a summer-long day camp in the gym provide a place for children of working parents. The gym hosts church dinners and fellowship activities. The congregation has come to view itself as consisting of two constituencies—the first originating in baptism and church membership and the second encompassing the people of the community.

None of these activities seems unusual. Many congregations have lots of children and maintain an active program to serve the larger community. The differences, however, are visible. Several provide clues to an education that nurtures hope.

EDUCATIONAL TASKS FOR HOPE

1. Church education nurtures hope if it equips children, youth, and adults to participate in the congregation's vocation in the world. The turning point in Community Church occurred when its members began to redirect their attention from activities designed to enrich their own common life or to preserve the congregation's heritage to the transformation of the structures and attitudes in the larger community that threatened to demean human life and experience both in the church and the neighborhood. Theologically, they redirected their energies to serving their neighbors. They discovered reason for hope in the act of expending themselves for the sake of the larger community. This does not mean that old patterns of racism, agism, sexism, and classism have not continued to intrude upon the relationships of Community Church members. It does mean that as they sought to understand what it means to "stabilize the community" they found themselves caught up in a mission that transforms in their own experience the destructive dynamics of these social forces. Their hope in a viable future has its origins in their consciousness of and commitment to the vocation of their congregation.[6]

2. Church education nurtures hope when it creates space for people to practice the transforming presence of God in the world. Most churches engage people in service projects—short-term and limited activities, which in fact may help alleviate human suffering, pain, and deprivation. But these service projects tend to be seen as elective parts of a congregation's program. They involve the discretionary use of member time, money, and commitments. Rarely do they inspire people to participate in the transformation of dehumanizing forces and structures. Community Church discovered something deeper. To be in mission involved the redirection of the energy and commitment of the whole congregation to that task. As a small congregation Community Church could not afford the luxury of sponsoring a range of activities simply to keep the interest of its membership. Even the annual Easter Egg hunt is not a party for the children of the church, but an opportunity to gather all the children of the neighborhood into relationships with adults whose presence conveys a sense of trust in their future.

3. Church education nurtures hope when it discovers clues to the content of the church's mission in its own faith responses. Perhaps the most important insight we can obtain from the experience of Community Church derives from the gradual realization of its members that the model for their efforts at "stabilization" did not come from political and social theories about human community—although they were often useful—but from the biblical vision of community encompassing all nations, races, classes, ages, and conditions of being human. It is a vision that honors difference and solidarity. Perhaps the paradigmatic event is Pentecost, when people experienced the unity of the Holy Spirit in their own tongues. Community Church has discovered that age, racial, and cultural differences are not threats to community but significant resources to the solidarity feeding the hope that can penetrate and dissolve despair.

4. Church education nurtures hope when it involves the playful exercise of the imagination. The capacity to dream dreams and to envision possibilities for the future of a congregation's life is dependent upon the development of congregational imagination. Imagination gives form to reality. It "takes what we sense and shapes it, giving it form and content. It provides the symbols which resonate with the reality" we have experienced. It lies at the heart of all things religious. Without imagination we could not recognize the wonder in mystery. Without imagination we would not recognize the presence of holiness. Without imagination we could not apprehend the connectedness of everyone and everything in the universe.[7]

The imagination feeds our sense of anticipation for the possibilities in our actions. And it provides the impetus to think new thoughts about those things that lie beyond our knowing. It makes poets of people who do not believe they have any faculty with language. It makes artists of people who do not know what to do with a paintbrush. It makes theologians of people who are not seminary scholars, but whose lives are filled with the power of the mystery of God. Imaginative playfulness led Community Church members to believe they could build a community center despite the limitations of the size of their membership and their financial resources. It is evident in a congregational commitment to children in a weekday program primarily sustained by volunteers and in the influence of church members on local public school policies. It certainly can be seen any afternoon or evening in the gym as volunteers from the church interact with people from many miles around. It currently enlivens an emerging vision of a day care center for the elderly in the community. This small congregation thinks big because its members experience the freedom to imagine what most congregations would consider to be impossible. The freedom to imagine leads them to explore the edges of God's grace for clues to the vision they see in their own experience of God for the total community.

The exercise of the imagination suffers in church education. It suffers whenever congregations seek curriculum resources that confine education to workbook activities for children or rote learning for adults. It suffers whenever congregations allow themselves to be satisfied with sedentary worship and anecdotal preaching. It suffers whenever congregations do not engage the subjects of their mission as agents of God's transforming grace in their lives. And it suffers whenever congregations fall victim to the notion sweeping the land that imagination is the work of the devil. The imagination is God's gift for human expectation. That gift is the resource to the human embrace of the mystery of God and the capacity to live with faith into the unknown future. Without imagination we become victims of the tyranny of the experience of people in power. Without imagination we miss hearing the still, small voice bringing messages of hope and salvation. Without imagination we cannot recognize the movement of the Spirit. Without imagination we do not see Christ in our neighbor.

EXERCISE IN CONGREGATIONAL ANALYSIS

Answer the following questions in an attempt to identify understandings and skills among the high school seniors in your congregation that contribute to a sense of hope. After reviewing the questions, identify the strengths and problems in the education of your church in nurturing hope among the church's youth.

CHURCH EDUCATION FOR HOPE INVENTORY

1. When and where have your high school seniors practiced discerning the evidence of God at work in their lives and their world in and through the life and ministry of the church?

2. When and where have your high school seniors had the opportunity to analyze and challenge oppressive and unjust social, political, and economic forces in the church, your community, and state as a part of their Christian education and service experiences in the church?

3. When and where have your high school seniors had

the opportunity to practice the skills of hospitality and caring for others? Do they use them naturally with persons of all ages and from a variety of cultural and socioeconomic backgrounds?

4. What experience do your high school seniors have in caring for those who are hurting, marginalized, oppressed? What patterns of stewardship reveal their commitment to the ministry of the church and their care for the earth?

5. When and where have your high school seniors practiced under the guidance of the church how to challenge those forces in school, work, and sometimes in their families that attempt to dehumanize and demean humanity?

TEACHING FOR HOPE

This is not the first time in human history in which the modes of ministry seem out of kilter with the circumstances of people. The crisis we face is no more extraordinary than that faced by the Jews in Babylon when the continuity of their faith traditions could no longer rely upon the political embodiment of God's promises. It is no more challenging than that faced by the early church as it sought under tremendous odds to incorporate a culturally and religiously diverse population into a new faith community. It is no more demanding than the task facing John and Charles Wesley as they sought to organize communities recruited from the mines and streets into methodistical societies of discipline and faith at the edge of both the Enlightenment and the Industrial Revolution.

In these historic experiences of being up against the loss of hope, we may discern the importance of the memory of the community of faith as the repository of images opening up the future. In exile in Babylon the Jews discovered clues to their future in the stories of the Exodus. The early church discovered clues to a new kind of community in the prophetic visions of Isaiah and Micah. The Wesleys discovered clues to the mission of the church in the disciplined servanthood of Jesus for the sake of the sick, the poor, the imprisoned, and the outcast.

In our own day we too may find power in the visionary images and metaphors of our ancestors of faith. My hunch, however, is that we will find even more powerful clues in the teaching roles of those who stood at the edge of communal despair to discern a new future. In the biblical witness two roles have caught my attention. They were often interchangeable. They were both visionary. One gathers up the teaching function of the prophet and the other, the poet. Over and over again we see the interplay of these two teaching roles in Isaiah, Jeremiah, some of the psalmists, the minor prophets, and the writers of the Gospels. Note the words of Isaiah:

> A voice cries out:
>
> "In the wilderness prepare the
>   way of the LORD,
>   make straight in the desert a
>   highway for our God.
> Every valley shall be lifted up,
>   and every mountain and hill
>   be made low;
> the uneven ground shall become
>   level,
>   and the rough places a plain.
> Then the glory of the LORD shall
>   be revealed,
>   and all the people shall see it
>   together."
>
> (Isa. 40:3-5)

Or the words of Luke:

> And Mary said,
> "My soul magnifies the Lord,
>   and my spirit rejoices in God
>   my Savior, . . .
> For the Mighty One . . .
>   . . . has scattered the proud in
>   the thoughts of their
>   hearts.
>   . . . has brought down the
>   powerful from their
>   thrones,
>   and lifted up the lowly;
>   . . . has filled the hungry with
>   good things,
>   and sent the rich away empty."
>   (Luke 1:46-53)

Passages such as these speak truth about our human condition. They also catch our imagination. They expand our horizons. They lift our spirits. They sponsor hope within community.

In a small but powerful way we can see the dynamics of prophetic and artistic teaching at work in the efforts of Community Church to live out the commission to be the Body of Christ in its neighborhood. Perhaps the basic gift of teaching for hope that one discovers at work in Community Church is *the discernment of possibility* where most people only see the loss of possibility. This is the aesthetic vision that informs the work of both prophet and artist. The pastor first, then others, began to discern seeds for their future in the social turbulence of their own community. Theologically, they began to look for God at work not in the familiar but in the unfamiliar. The pastor saw that possibility in the most obvious resource to be found in most places: the children of the neighborhood.

Although her discovery is reminiscent of the teachings of Jesus, it is not a particularly convincing one in the discussions of churches and governmental agencies today. After the entertainment value of children has worn out, all too many become liabilities to parents and the agencies of the community that serve them. We deprive them of the physical necessities they need to be healthy. We warehouse them in large and impersonal school buildings. We deprive them of adequate nurturing adult relationships. We allow television and a host of peer group activities structured by adults to consume their time and attention. But through children Community Church began to envision a new future. The stained glass window of black and white children in the arms of Jesus holds up that vision. The active participation of children and youth in worship celebrates it. The after school program embodies it. Older members of the church discern in these children the future leadership of the community. This congregation's investment in children is a way of accepting responsibility now for the shape of the future.

A second characteristic of teachers who nurture hope in congregations for a viable future may be found in their *willingness to risk the status quo*. Prophets and artists are audacious. They challenge the conventions. Indeed, they refuse to be bound by conventional knowledge, perceptions, or practices. Rollo May puts it even more boldly. They embody the courage to "do battle with the gods"— the false gods that dominate the allegiance of people and blind them to the reality in which they exist.[8] This means teachers who nurture hope unmask the efforts of people and institutions to mystify the truth of their experience and to disguise the real possibilities that lie before them.

Challenging the conventions is a common theme in the life of Community Church. Without any clue as to the source of the funds needed, church leaders and members decided to build a gym where people of all races would be welcomed. In an era when people claim they do not have time to volunteer their time, the basic ministries of this congregation depend upon the volunteer commitment of many hours a week to sustain its mission to the larger community. They cannot afford to hire someone else to do their work. They challenged the conventions of the school system to create a safer environment for their children. And perhaps most significantly, they have challenged so far the convention that a congregation in the southeastern United States can gather black and white people into the mutuality of living in community with one another. Their commitment to the celebration of ethnic, racial, and cultural diversity profoundly exemplifies a different kind of community from what most people know.

A third characteristic of teachers who nurture hope in congregations for a viable future is found in their invitation to others to *participate in the work of creating an alternative future*. The primary role of the pastor in the creation of a community of hope in this congregation cannot be overestimated. If we looked no deeper, however, we would conclude that the teaching role of the prophet or artist is a solitary one. At this point we may begin to recover the biblical notion of the work of the prophet. Most were teachers. Students gathered to learn from the prophet. They practiced discerning the interaction of God and the world in the manner of the prophet. And after the prophet's death they continued the work of the prophet but in relation to the circumstances in which they now found themselves. They did not become slaves to the prophet's words but agents of the prophetic tradition. They immersed themselves in that tradition to the point where they participated in its creative extension into the future. Such is the work of the teacher as prophet or artist.

This dynamic is clearly at work at Community Church. The vision of a stable faith community modeling intergenerational and interracial dynamics becomes the impetus to its mission in the larger community. A recent example may be seen in the way one of the women of the congregation has discovered her own vocation within the congregational vocation in the community. The idea that the church could become a center for all aging members of the larger community and at the same time a primary center of care for young children has seized her imagination and now informs the way she lives. It has "pulled" her back into graduate school to obtain the requisite educational preparation. It has inspired her to begin developing plans. It has led her to begin sharing her dreams and ideas with others. The idea may have originated in a conversation or comment of the pastor some time ago. But this woman is now clearly the agent of this part of the congregation's mission. She has assumed responsibility for embodying the congregation's hope for a vital and stable community.

Her role in the life of Community Church may expand our notion of teaching. Its impetus and authority are located in the interplay of her vocation with that of the congregation. This contrasts with the typical perspective that views teaching as integral to a church program or school structure. She teaches whenever and wherever people have a question or express an interest in discovering what she is learning or planning to do. These actions often lead to the formation of groups seeking to learn more or to respond with the power of what they have learned.

We can see similar patterns at work in those congregations that truly nurture an artistic vision in their worship and common life. It creates an environment where poets, painters, songwriters, composers, liturgists, and many others find a place to express and test their vision for the new creation taking shape in the congregation's midst. Northside Church provides a good example. The building celebrated the creativity of its members. Banners were created for each liturgical season. Members composed music for worship. Children wrote prayers and poems to be shared with the entire congregation. Youth contributed to the development and production of dramatic productions. Its members included jazz artists who created liturgical services encompassing this art form. The congregation did not buy flowers from a florist; instead members created altar arrangements reflecting the symbols and meanings of the liturgical seasons. Many of the people who engaged in these activities were not professional artists. Instead they were invited by the congregation into an activity of creating for the praise of God.

These congregations discerned hope through their prophetic and creative engagement with the mystery of God at the edges of their experience. The burden of the modern age, the silence of God in the face of the overwhelming dynamics of contemporary life, the fear of the unknown became not blocks to congregational life, but the point of departure for a grand adventure into the mystery through which we may faintly and dimly discern sources of hope. Again we see an education centered around the events of worship and mission. Education cannot be contained in classrooms or limited to the school of the church, as important as the teaching and learning in these settings may be. Instead, hope is nurtured in the course of a congregation's engagement in God's vocation of emancipating creation. Consequently, educating for hope occurs as congregations order their lives to participate in this transformational activity.

EXERCISE IN CONGREGATIONAL ANALYSIS

Identify where you see prophetic and artistic teaching in your congregation. What helps or hinders their effectiveness as sources of hope for the membership of your congregation?

A Guide to Revisioning Local Church Education

So FAR WE HAVE MADE several claims for the future of local church education.

1. Existing approaches to church education are no longer adequate for the task of building up communities of faith to praise God and serve neighbor for the emancipatory transformation of the world.

2. With increasing demands on limited resources, the education in different congregations will be linked more by the participation of their members in shared events of the Christian story than by denominational strategies for church education, curriculum resources, or leadership training programs.

3. In our increasingly pluralistic world, congregations can no longer assume that their values and commitments will be taught and/or reinforced by other educational institutions in their larger communities.

4. If congregations are to become communities of praise and service for the sake of God's transformation of the world, they must assume primary responsibility for the education of people into the responsible embodiment of those ministries.

5. Three tasks central to this educational venture include:

136

a) building communities of faith in and through which discipleship to Jesus Christ is nurtured;

b) building communities of faith capable of helping people make religious sense of their encounters between their traditions of faith and the explosion of new knowledge that surrounds them, the changing circumstances of their lives, and the decisions they must make for living into a changing world;

c) building communities of faith capable of nurturing hope vital enough to invite people into the human vocation of praising God and serving neighbor for the sake of the transformation of the world.

We now reach that point in our study when we must ask what such a religious education might look like. Lawrence Cremin has reminded us of an important distinction to guide this discussion. People are constantly learning. Much of our learning does not take place in classrooms, workshops, retreats, or conferences. We learn from television and radio. We learn from reading. We learn by observing what is going on around us. We learn in conversation. We learn from people who would never describe themselves as teachers.

But some of our learning does occur through structures designed for teaching and learning guided by teachers trained specifically for that task. Cremin has observed that these "formal" educational settings have three characteristics relevant to our discussion.

First, they are deliberate or **intentional.** When congregations as communities of faith organize their lives to help people enter into their ministries of worship and mission with a spirit of freedom and competence, they intend that people will learn to act in certain ways, be familiar with certain things, discern certain meanings, take on certain values and sensibilities, and assume certain commitments. To do less limits the quality and character of our participation in the primary events that give order and purpose to congregational life and mission.

Second, they are **systematic.** Certain learnings must precede others. Some learnings build on others. Some learnings emerge from the exercise of other learnings. When congregations organize their lives as communities of faith to assist people in formulating questions to integrate their quests for faith and understanding and find the resources to assist them in this quest, they establish procedures to intensify and deepen the significance of their experience. These efforts are crucial if people are to make sense or meaning from their experience and relationships, their encounters with the stories and vision of Christian faith, their consciousness of human pain and suffering and their participation in the worship and mission of the congregation.

Third, an intentional and systematic religious education, if effective, is also **sustained** over time.[1] If the people of a congregation are to extend the memory of the church's story and vision into the future, specific learning tasks must be repeated until they become so familiar we do not have to think about them. At that point we are so embedded in them they shape our perceptions and expectations. If those memories are to be relevant, however, their nurture must be sustained over enough time to be integrated into our developing capacities for comprehension and meaning and to be recast and reinterpreted for the new circumstances and situations in which congregations find themselves.

So what does an intentional, systematic, and sustained congregational education centered around its primary worship and mission events look like? No single answer suffices. Although congregations share many common Christian ideas, values, and practices (especially within denominations), differences in membership, settings (with their distinctive economic, political, and social dynamics), and local faith traditions heighten their particularity. But one can discern a similar educational process at work in quite different communities of faith. The three elements common to all successful educational ministries were described in the second chapter: (1) the intentional and systematic **preparation** of people for worship and mission; (2) the **engagement** of people in celebrative actions of worship and self-giving actions of service or mission; and (3) the intentional and systematic **critical reflection** on the faithfulness and relevance of the congregation's worship and mission and the preparation people received to participate in them. Learning is sustained in this process through the repetition of congregational efforts to prepare people for participating in an event, engaging people in that event, and reflecting critically with people on its significance for the church in its vocation of living into the transformational activity of God.

In event-full education, some **teaching/learning groups** may be organized according to age. Many will be intergenerational. Some may be organized according to interest or ability. Others may be organized in relation to specific commitments or concerns. Some may be existing groups in the congregation. Others may include people from other congregations or community groups. Age or interest, however, are not the primary criteria for the creation of teaching/learning groups as they are in the church's schools. Instead, a teaching/learning setting will consist of those people who need to know something to participate in specific acts of praise and mission.

The **setting** for teaching and learning will depend on the task to be undertaken and the time needed for learning. It may occur in a classroom, church sanctuary, choir room, social service agency, factory cafeteria, home, or hospital room—wherever, in fact, people gather to prepare or to reflect on some event and their participation in it.

Teachers in event-full education include those persons who facilitate any activity or process designed to help people *prepare* themselves to *engage* in events of worship and/or service and to *reflect* critically on their experience. Teachers are related more to specific functions of the community than to specified age or interest groups. Some will be teaching people new songs and hymns. Some will be rehearsing liturgical or dramatic moments. Some will be guiding people through historical and theological sources and interpretations of the event. Some will be supervising the practice of people to ensure the competency of their participation. Some will help people discover in their experience connections to an event in the past or in different circumstances. This last teaching function may well be the one most often missing in congregational life and special efforts may be needed to identify people and times when critical reflection might occur.

The **curriculum** for teaching and learning emerges from the interplay of historic texts (biblical and theological) that illumine the events and relationships that structure our corporate experience and the questions and issues that a congregation faces as it seeks to engage faithfully in worship and service. Curriculum resources based on the lectionary or the cycle of texts guiding the International Lesson Series are designed to facilitate the preparation of people to participate in the significant events of the church year. Other resources may be developed or selected by local church committees for specific events.

GETTING ORGANIZED

In the following section we begin to make use of the study we have just concluded. You will find suggestions for assessing the information gathered while reading the book, thoughts about recasting certain programs and structures that currently contain the congregation's education, and a plan for thinking in new ways to educate persons for worship and mission.

A task force or committee should be appointed to make recommendations and to implement the findings from this study. It should include a core group of persons who have read and discussed the book. The work of the task force will be based on the information collected while reading the previous chapters. It may include assigning questions and issues to other groups in the congregation to broaden the numbers of people involved in this study of the congregation's educational future.

The following exercises are suggested as a guide to the work of the task force. Other ways of assessing the data and revisioning the congregation's education suggested by task force members may be more helpful to their studies. The specific process is not as important as the task itself. Groups engaging in this process should plan to spend anywhere from four weeks to six months working through the issues and possibilities for the future of the congregation's education.

STEP I: Gathering and Reviewing Data

Exercise 1: Prepare for the first task force meeting.

This step should occur prior to any session of the task force. The material collected during each of the exercises in the previous five chapters should be reproduced in a form that task force members can use. Make copies of the information collected for everyone on the task force. Summaries of this information might be published in a weekly newsletter or bulletin to inform the congregation of the work of the task force.

Exercise 2: Identify strengths and problems in the congregation's education.

Take six sheets of newsprint. On three sheets write at the top the word *strengths*. Below the word *strengths* write "Building Community" on one sheet, "Making Meaning" on a second sheet, and "Discerning Hope" on the third sheet. On the other three sheets write the word *problems*. Then add the three headings on community, meaning, and hope under it. As the task force reviews the information collected for each exercise identify specific strengths and problems in the way your congregation educates people for worship and mission. If you do not have newsprint, a large blackboard will do. The chart you create may look something like this:

Assessment of the Effectiveness of Our Congregation's Education

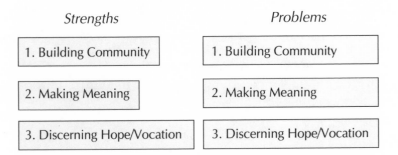

Strengths	Problems
1. Building Community	1. Building Community
2. Making Meaning	2. Making Meaning
3. Discerning Hope/Vocation	3. Discerning Hope/Vocation

An example of a strength might be the dedication of teachers in classes for younger children. An example of a problem might be the inconsistent attendance of youth in study programs. Hold this information and move on to the next exercise.

Exercise 3: Identify paradigmatic events for congregational identity and mission.

1. In your review of the congregation's education, list the words that seem to be most commonly used to describe what makes the life and work of the congregation important to people.

2. Then list the stories that seem to be most commonly told to illustrate or clarify the life and work of the congregation.

3. When these lists are completed, review them for themes and stories in church or biblical tradition evoked by those words and stories. For example, do the words and stories emphasize fellowship, reconciliation, covenant, or something else? Are the words and stories that seem central now different from those that seemed central ten or fifty years ago?

4. As you discuss these questions, see if you can create a *Trajectory of Events* from contemporary back to biblical times. It may reveal how the life and work of the congregation participates in and extends the meaning of those ancient stories into the present. An example based on a congregation's annual covenant renewal service might look like the following:

A PROCESS FOR DISCOVERING ROOTS OF CONTEMPORARY EXPERIENCE AND IDENTITY IN THE PAST

Stories of Annual Covenant Service	Stories of baptisms and confirmations	Stories of creating congregational covenant	Stories of covenants in the denomination	Bible stories of covenants

A PROCESS FOR DISCOVERING CLUES FOR THE FUTURE IN THE PAST

5. Before leaving this exercise, list significant stories from the Bible and church tradition omitted from your list. Explore with one another how important these sto-

ries might be to the congregation's image of itself if people knew them. This activity might lead you to suggest events and their stories that need to be emphasized in the future. Examples might include preparing your congregation to participate in Pentecost, assessing its relationship to children who play in the streets around the church building in light of the view of children in the Kingdom of God portrayed in the Gospels, or developing a strategy to help your congregation take more responsibility for their care of the environment.

You may not find it easy to identify words and stories that seem to describe your congregation's identity and mission. If this is the case, you may need to work through Exercise 4 before returning to the tasks of exploring what paradigmatic events distinctively inform the life and mission of your congregation.

Exercise 4: Assess ways people are prepared to participate in congregational events.

For this exercise you will need the time line of seasonal, occasional, and unexpected events created while reading chapter 2. The steps in this exercise are outlined below.

1. Review each event on the time line. In small letters above each event describe as concretely as possible *when* and *how* the congregation prepares people to participate competently in the event. For example, as you look at the event of weekly worship you may have a worship readiness class for children that helps children learn the words to hymns and prayers prior to their participation in given worship services. Perhaps choir programs help some people practice the music for worship. Perhaps the pastor meets with people to study the sermon text for the following Sunday. In a similar way examine when and how people are prepared to participate in some missional activity. This may involve an orientation by the people being served. It may involve a study of the eco-

nomic or political issues integral to the mission project. It may involve practicing the skills required in the missional activity. After completing this task decide which events involve adequate preparation and which do not.

2. Below the time line of events write in things the congregation does to help people make sense of their experience of the event. For example, your congregation might have a session on Sunday evenings when people might discuss the morning's sermon with the pastor. Or at the end of a mission activity a session may be planned for people to share the meaning of the experience with others in the congregation and to explore what they have learned about responding to God's call to participate in God's transforming activity.

3. When you have completed filling in this information, identify any events or clusters of events that are especially important to the people of the congregation, involve extensive preparation, and are marked by significant reflection on their meanings. Explore ways the education for these events illumines paradigmatic events in Christian history that underlie the identity and vocation of your congregation. If you were unable to identify any central events in the previous exercise, you may now have enough information to create a *Trajectory of Events* around this new information. Be sure to identify other words and stories from our theological and biblical traditions that fill in the meanings of these events.

You have now gathered a lot of information. It is time to move on to the next step in the process of revisioning the education for your congregation.

STEP II: Making Decisions about the Future of Church Education

Exercise 1: Think about educating for weekly worship.

Since this is the central event in every congregation's life, let's begin here. Several questions might guide your thinking about the education the people in your congregation need to participate competently in this event. On a large sheet of newsprint or on a blackboard list the following questions and then work through each of them in order.

Content. *What do people need to know to participate freely and competently in the worship of this congregation?* The task may sound big, but it really involves many small things, such as whether it is important to know how to use the worship bulletin or be familiar with a new hymn tune before singing it. In other words, it is important to be very specific. Begin by going through a copy of the order of worship in your congregation. Then ask yourselves how important is it for people to be familiar with the hymns, corporate prayers and responses before using them in worship each week? How do newcomers discover whether people in your congregation kneel, stand, or sit during prayers or how you receive the communion elements? The lack of such information can create a sense of estrangement in the people who visit our congregations.

How important is it that people be familiar with the biblical texts that inform the sermon? Does it make any difference to the quality and character of the worship service if people know one another or not? Is there any difference in the kind of familiarity you should expect of children, youth, and adults with the parts of worship? You may end up asking other questions like these as you think about helping people enter fully into the spirit of corporate worship.

Setting. *Of those parts of worship with which people are quite familiar, where are they learning them?* Are there other places that might be used for this purpose? For example, some congregations are discovering that with erratic attendance patterns a more effective use of the Sunday morning church school hour has been to use that time to prepare people for the worship that follows. Hymns are practiced. Written prayers are read and interpreted.

The scripture texts are discussed and placed in historical context in ways that are appropriate to the learning styles of children, youth, and adults. Concerns of people about the circumstances and issues of the church and community are examined. In smaller congregations this preparation time could occur in intergenerational formats led by a pastor or layperson. This experience may remind older members of Sunday school opening exercises popular in many congregations several years ago.

Other congregations are discovering that a given night a week turned over to choir rehearsals, Bible study, and congregational fellowship becomes an optimal time to prepare people for Sunday morning worship. Long ago the staff of East Harlem Protestant Parish used a similar weekday Bible study time to prepare themselves to preach on Sunday morning. The sermons grew out of the congregation's study of the weekly scripture texts.

Leadership. Affecting when and where the preparation for worship should occur is the availability of those persons best equipped to do the teaching or leading. So the next step in thinking about education for worship should consider *who can provide leadership to these activities of learning.* Perhaps the pastor or Christian educator on a congregation's staff will need to meet with these persons on a monthly basis to prepare them for their teaching.

Curriculum. This approach to a congregation's education advocates a much closer relationship between preaching and teaching than is often the case. This may help clarify questions about *what kinds of educational resources are needed* for those times and places when people are preparing for worship. If the pastor of your congregation follows the lectionary, curriculum resources that follow the lectionary may be useful. The preacher may be interested in organizing study notes of a text in such a way that they might become the curriculum for educational settings with youth and adults. In congregations that use the International Lesson Series in their Sunday schools, a preacher may choose to organize a preaching schedule around its selection of scripture readings.

Whatever is chosen should enhance the engagement of congregation and preacher in the study of common texts. But worship is more than scripture readings and sermons. Resources to explore the background and meaning of the creeds, the liturgical seasons, the sacraments, and the elements of the liturgy may be important to acquire or develop. The hymnal and a commentary on hymns may become important texts as well.

Critical Reflection. The last question to be asked is *when and where do people have the opportunity to talk about the meaning of worship and the decisions those meanings might be leading them to make.* So now it becomes important to ask when and where people might be encouraged to reflect, assess, and put into some theological context their meanings from participation in worship. When and where will they articulate issues for further exploration and identify decisions people make in response to their worship and study experiences? What support do people have for making changes in their lives when they discover some new claim of the gospel on their lives? Where do they have the opportunity to explore the significance of their experience in worship for the routines and relationships of family life, work, civic life, and leisure time? These questions may need to be asked when the task force begins to identify other times and places in the weekly schedule for this dimension of a congregation's education.

Exercise 2: Think about educating for mission.

After answering these four questions, repeat the process in relation to a mission project or emphasis in the congregation. The task may be more difficult because few congregations have directly related service to Sunday worship. Congregational mission tends to be identified with a budget item or with the altruistic activities of individuals or small groups. Notable exceptions may be found in congregations that gave leadership to the Civil Rights or peace movements, gave hospitality to the homeless or disenfranchised in their neighborhoods, or challenged governmental or church policies regarding the role and place of women. When service to neighbor (including care for the quality of the neighbor's environment) is viewed as the necessary counterpoint to congregational worship, considerably more attention will need to be given to preparing people to participate in that effort.

The questions to assess the adequacy of a congregation's preparation for its mission also include:

1. What do people need to know or know how to do in order to participate freely and competently in this mission event?

2. When is the optimal time and where is the best place for people to prepare themselves to participate in this missional activity or emphasis?

3. Who are the people who can provide leadership for those educational experiences?

4. What resources are needed to help teachers and participants in that learning process?

5. Where do people have the opportunity to explore the meanings and claims on their lives from their participation in this mission event?

After reviewing your answers to these five questions, identify strengths and problems in your congregation's education of its members for participation in ministries of care for others. Your answers to these questions may lead you to make some recommendations for any group in the congregation planning a missional event or emphasis.

Exercise 3: Think about educating for seasonal events.

The next step will be to review the primary seasonal events of worship and mission and go through a similar process for each. As the group begins to work through this process it should make visible existing ways the congregation prepares people for such events as Advent, Epiphany, Lent, Homecoming Sunday, or the fall revival. It should also begin to make visible the rhythmic patterns involving the movement from intense preparation to engagement in an event to reflection on that event through the year. Identify seasonal events in which more emphasis on educating people is needed to help them participate in them more fully or to reflect on their experience of the season.

Exercise 4: Think about educating for occasional events.

The educational venture of a congregation may be intensified as it takes these same questions and begins to identify how they help people enter into the occasional events of worship and mission freely and competently. Begin by reviewing the list of occasional events from your time line. Add other events that may not have been included. Review the kinds of preparation and critical reflection people experience for each of these occasional events. Clearly established educational patterns may be in place for baptism, confirmation, weddings, and work camps. Ask yourselves if they actually prepare people to participate in them or to reflect critically on their experience of them. Other occasional events may not have any form of preparation or reflection on their meanings. These events may then become the subject of some planning around how people might be empowered to experience their potential as sources of faith and mission.

Exercise 5: Think about educating for unexpected events.

Most congregations do not attend to the importance of having in place an educational approach to the unexpected events that occur in the lives of people, congregations, and communities. But I would like to suggest that this step is also important in revisioning a congregation's education. I think of a congregation that had developed a process to prepare its members for a major missional project in its city and then discovered that the same process effectively prepared its members to provide leadership to the larger community when much of it was destroyed by floodwaters. In this instance, the congregation had in place a process for analyzing an unexpected situation, interpreting that situation in light of the gospel, and identifying actions that might embody the gospel for those who were left as victims. What process might be most appropriate for your congregation?

STEP III: Making Decisions about Educational Structures for Event-Full Education

In an event-full education the Sunday school, RCIA, or Disciple Bible[2] study programs, youth groups, Wednesday night Bible studies and other traditional educational structures need not be eliminated. In fact, the opposite may well be true. These educational options may actually make important contributions to the processes of building community, making meaning, and discerning hope in the life of a congregation if redirected to equipping people to participate in significant church events. For example, RCIA or Disciple Bible study may help people discover new possibilities for their faith journeys which then become preparation for the basic events of congregational life. Sunday school classes that are not recast as times of preparation for specific events of worship and mission may become occasions for enriching the education people receive elsewhere in the life of the congregation. Enrichment education becomes valuable if it, in fact, enriches the education normally received elsewhere.

The process of revisioning congregational education may lead many congregations to redirect the purposes of choir practices to the preparation for participation in worship rather than the performance of music in worship. The Sunday school or other weekday education might become occasions for engaging the texts and practicing the readings for worship. Committee meetings might become occasions for study to inform congregational actions as well as to reflect critically on their significance.

The process of revisioning congregational education may also lead to some radical new forms of congregational life. Some small and mid-size congregations, for example, have begun to move to a flexible two- to three-hour block of time on the day of worship. Part of that time is spent in age-level and intergenerational activities to prepare people for the worship of the morning and missional events of the week. Part of that time engages people in the act of worship. Part of the time includes an opportunity for people to ask questions and to talk with one another about implications from their encounter with the gospel during the past week for their lives.

The process of revisioning congregational education may lead some congregations—especially those with a membership made up of people who often have to work on Sundays—to think of totally different schedules for the primary events in their common life. I think, for example, of urban Protestant congregations that include weekly worship on some other day of the week or of the many congregations that are beginning to hold much of their education on a Tuesday or Wednesday night, or as is common in many African American congregations, on Saturdays.

As you begin to make decisions about the future of the education of your church in building community, making meaning, and discerning hope, the focus of your efforts should always be developing an education that nurtures Christian identity and resources Christian mission. The time has come to begin making decisions about the future shape of education in your congregation.

Exercise 1: Develop an educational planning guide for congregational events.

The most basic task is to establish a planning guide for the committees of your congregation so that as they plan an event, they will include in that plan, educational steps to help people participate in the event freely and competently, and opportunities for people to assess the meaning of their experience in the event in the light of Christian tradition and the realities of their daily lives. You may develop a worksheet similar to the one below or you may adapt this one.

Planning Guide for Congregational Events

1. Event
2. Date and time
3. Place to be held
4. Purpose of the event
5. Who is expected to participate?
6. Design of the event
7. What biblical texts, theological ideas, historical figures and events, liturgical materials, hymns, or other information do people need to know to participate fully in the event?
8. When and where will people be introduced to these materials?
9. Who will provide the leadership for these educational activities? What training will they need?
10. When and where will people have the opportunity to reflect on the meaning of the event?
11. How will people be informed of the event and of the educational activities associated with it?

Exercise 2: Establish priorities for congregational education.

Perhaps the most important task in planning for event-full education in your congregation occurs in prioritizing which events should be supported by major educational efforts. The emphasis on preparing people for Christmas and Easter through the seasons of Advent and Lent in most congregations would indicate that most congregations have already begun this process. The lack of attention given to preparing people for Sunday morning worship or for some major mission emphasis might mean more attention needs to be given to them.

One way to establish the educational priorities for your congregation would be to go back to the lists of seasonal, occasional, and unexpected events. Go through the lists with three different colored pens. With one pen mark those events with adequate educational efforts. With a second pen mark those events that need to be given more ongoing emphasis. With the third pen mark those events that would benefit from a focused occasional educational effort.

You should now be ready to report your insights from the study of your congregation's education and recommendations for congregational action. Identify what you would want to communicate to the congregation and list the recommendations you would like to make. Decide who will present the task force report. Then find some way to celebrate the work you have done together.

A FINAL WORD

If you have followed all the steps outlined in this chapter, you have been engaged in a rigorous study of your congregation's education. It is my hope that it will lead to a renewed sense of vitality in the worship and mission life of your congregation. The education of a community can never be taken for granted. Perhaps this is especially true as we find ourselves at the edge of the twenty-first century. In the face of rapid change, multiple values, and many options for our commitments, the challenge to congregations to educate their members for participation in God's transformative activity is even more urgent.

May your efforts be filled with joy and blessing.

Notes

INTRODUCTION

1. Quoted in J. Philip Wogaman, *Faith and Fragmentation: Christianity for a New Age* (Philadelphia: Fortress Press, 1985), p. 3.

2. Maria Harris also uses this metaphor to frame her thoughtful discussion of church curriculum in *Fashion Me a People: Curriculum in the Church* (Louisville: Westminster/John Knox, 1989), p. 13.

3. Cf. James D. Smart, *The Teaching Ministry of the Church: An Examination of the Basic Principles of Christian Education* (Philadelphia: The Westminster Press, 1954); John H. Westerhoff III, *Will Our Children Have Faith?* (New York: The Seabury Press, 1976); John M. Hull, *What Prevents Christian Adults from Learning?* (Philadelphia: Trinity Press International, 1991 [1985]); Peter Benson and Carolyn H. Eklin, *Effective Christian Education: A National Study of Protestant Congregations* (Minneapolis: Search Institute, 1990); Rebecca S. Chopp, *The Power To Speak: Feminism, Language, God* (New York: The Crossroad Publishing Company, 1991).

4. I have borrowed this term from my colleague Rebecca Chopp, who envisions a transformation of discourse based on a "retrieval of the Protestant insistence on the living dynamic communication between God and world," challenging historically dominant voices with discourses originating from the margins of the church and world. Chopp's insights, based on a feminist hermeneutic, illumine the challenge to a church education that embraces the plurality of human experience and culture (pp. 3-5).

1. FLAWS IN THE CHURCH EDUCATION VESSEL

1. With appreciation to Elie Wiesel, whose story in the preface of *The Gates of the Forest* (New York: Holt, Rinehart and Winston, 1966 [1964]), inspired the story that follows.

2. Benson and Eklin, *Effective Christian Education*, pp. 3, 12-13.

3. Westerhoff, *Will Our Children Have Faith?* p. 2.

4. The names of people in the various stories throughout the book have been changed to ensure anonymity.

5. E. D. Hirsch, Jr., *Cultural Literacy: What Every American Needs to Know* (New York: Vintage Books, 1988), pp. xv, xvii.

6. Robert N. Bellah, Richard Madsen, William M. Sullivan, Ann Swidler, and Steven M. Tipton, *Habits of the Heart: Individualism and Commitment in American Life* (Berkeley: University of California Press, 1985), p. 65; Robert Wuthnow, *The Restructuring of American Religion* (Princeton: Princeton University Press, 1988), pp. 88, 171.

7. Class notes, Kahn interview, fall 1990, p. 5.

8. Edward Farley, *The Fragility of Knowledge: Theological Education in the Church and the University* (Philadelphia: Fortress Press, 1988), p. 85.

9. For an extended discussion of the shopping mall as a paradigm for contemporary secondary schooling, see Arthur G. Powell, Eleanor Farrar, and

David K. Cohen, *The Shopping Mall High School: Winners and Losers in the Educational Marketplace* (Boston: Houghton Mifflin Company, 1985), pp. 8-65.

10. These are images of education identified by Maxine Green in *Teacher as Stranger: Educational Philosophy for the Modern Age* (Belmont, Calif.: The Wadsworth Publishing Company, 1973), p. 3.

11. Bellah, et al., *Habits of the Heart*, pp. 82-83; John Fry, *A Hard Look at Adult Christian Education* (Philadelphia: The Westminster Press), p. 82.

12. For an extended discussion of these patterns in the education of the church, see Charles R. Foster, "Imperialism in the Education of the Church," *Religious Education* 86 (Winter 1991) 1:145-56.

13. Mrs. S. J. Brigham, "A Hard Task," *Picture Lesson Paper* XVI (March 22, 1885) 3D.

14. *1993 ESL Bilingual Catalogue* (Addison: Wesley), p. 37.

2. EVENTS THAT FORM AND TRANSFORM

1. Robert MacAfee Brown, *Is Faith Obsolete?* (Philadelphia: The Westminster Press, 1974), p. 28.

2. Cf. Joseph V. Crockett, *Teaching Scripture From an African-American Perspective* (Nashville: Discipleship Resources, 1990); Grant S. Shockley, "Christian Education and the Black Church" in Charles R. Foster, Ethel R. Johnson, and Grant S. Shockley, *Christian Education Journey of Black Americans: Past, Present, Future* (Nashville: Discipleship Resources, 1985), pp. 1-18.

3. Cf. C. Eric Lincoln and Lawrence H. Mimaya, *The Black Church in the African American Experience* (Durham: Duke University Press, 1990), pp. 310-12.

3. BUILDING COMMUNITY

1. *The United Methodist Hymnal* (Nashville: The United Methodist Publishing House, 1989), No. 333.

2. The Search Institute study of education in six denominations reported in *Effective Christian Education* (Minneapolis, 1990) identifies something of the diminishing effectiveness of church education. Perhaps the problem becomes more poignant in news reports similar to the one written by a reporter who, without apparent consciousness of the issue to which we refer, describes the visit of a group of Christians from a single denomination to Muslim Kazakhstan. After a meal their hosts began a traditional time of singing. The "only song" this group of U.S. Christians "knew in common by memory . . . was 'Kum Ba Yah.' " The author does not indicate whether or not the group eliminated songs focused on Jesus Christ out of sensitivity to the faith of their hosts. Even so, the lack of "familiarity" with other possibilities underscores my concern about a diminishing literacy in the vocabulary of the Christian faith—even among leaders of the church (Diane Huie Belay, "Nuclear 'ground zero' site for Christian song," The United Methodist *Reporter* 140 [Nov. 26, 1993] 26:3).

3. Charles R. Foster, *Teaching in the Community of Faith* (Nashville: Abingdon Press, 1982), pp. 17-18.

4. Stanley J. Hauerwas, *A Community of Character: Toward a Constructive Christian Social Ethic* (Notre Dame: University of Notre Dame Press, 1981), p. 1. I have a different image of the relationship of the church community to its social context than Hauerwas proposes. He advocates that if "Christians" are "to regain any significant sense of the polity that emerges from these two actions, then they must gain an appropriate sense of separateness" from the liberal social patterns that surround them (p. 2). Although he modifies the word *separateness* with the word *appropriate*, polities emphasizing separateness tend to reflect autonomous values rooted in assumptions that reality can be broken down into discrete parts. It can, without intending to do so, become the impetus to parochialism on the one hand and arrogance on the other. I would urge a more dynamic view—one that emphasizes the importance of the interplay of separateness (to maintain identity and vocation) and interaction (to celebrate the "God-givenness" of all creation). I prefer the image of the Christian community as "a servant people" whose presence is both visible and invisible.

5. Clarence Joseph Rivers, "The Oral African Tradition Versus the Ocular Western Tradition," *This Far by Faith: American Black Worship and Its African Roots* (Washington, D.C.: The National Office for Black Catholics and The Liturgical Conference, 1977), pp. 42-43.

6. Edward T. Hall, *The Dance of Life: The Other Dimension of Time* (Garden City, N.Y.: Anchor Press/Doubleday, 1983); Rivers, *This Far by Faith*, pp. 45-46.

7. See Paulo Freire, *The Pedagogy of the Oppressed* (New York: The Continuum Publishing Corp., 1970 [1968]), pp. 57ff., for a discussion of the contrast between banking and liberative education.

8. Walter Brueggemann, *The Creative Word: Canon as a Model for Biblical Education* (Philadelphia: Fortress Press, 1982), pp. 1, 14-15.

9. For an expanded discussion of the relationship of memory and vision, see Thomas H. Groome, *Christian Religious Education: Sharing Our Story and Vision* (San Francisco: Harper & Row, 1980), p. 192.

10. Letty Russell, *The Future of Partnership* (Philadelphia: The Westminster Press, 1979), p. 35.

11. Sharon Welch, "An Ethic of Solidarity and Difference," in Henry A. Giroux, ed., *Postmodernism, Feminism, and Cultural Politics: Redrawing Educational Boundaries* (Albany: State University of New York Press, 1991), p. 97; Chopp, *The Power to Speak*, pp. 6-9.

12. Henri J. M. Nouwen, *Reaching Out: The Three Movements of the Spiritual Life* (Garden City, N.Y.: Doubleday, 1975), p. 51.

13. Ibid., p. 69.

14. Brueggemann, *The Creative Word*, pp. 22-23.

15. Quoted in Foster, *Teaching in the Community of Faith*, pp. 33.

16. Cf. Groome, *Christian Religious Education*, for a discussion of the interplay of story and vision in framing the assumptions and strategies of a Christian religious education; also Jerome Berryman, *Godly Play: A Way of Religious Education* (San Francisco: Harper San Francisco, 1991), for a provocative discussion of a Christian religious education based on the stories in the play of children.

17. Westerhoff, *Will Our Children Have Faith?* pp. 96-97.

18. Cf. Kenneth Keniston and The Carnegie Council on Children, *All Our Children: The American Family Under Pressure* (New York: Harcourt Brace Jovanovich, 1977), pp. 17-23, for a discussion of the shift in parenting from

roles of nurturing to roles of managing the lives of children. Cf. also Mihaly Csikszentmihalyi and Reed Larson for a detailed study of the relationships and experiences among a selected group of teenagers in one high school. Notably absent from their study was any data indicating the presence of adult mentors or friends outside the family; *Being Adolescent: Conflict and Growth in the Teenage Years* (New York: Basic Books, 1984).

19. Parker Palmer, *To Know as We Are Known: A Spirituality of Education* (San Francisco: Harper & Row, 1983), p. 88.

4. MAKING MEANING

1. Cf. Sara Little, *To Set One's Heart: Belief and Teaching in the Church* (Atlanta: John Knox Press, 1983); Jack L. Seymour, Margaret Ann Crain, Joseph V. Crockett, *Educating Christians: The Intersection of Meaning, Learning, and Vocation* (Nashville: Abingdon Press, 1993) esp. chap. 7; Thomas H. Groome, *Sharing Faith: A Comprehensive Approach to Religious Education and Pastoral Ministry: The Way of Shared Praxis* (San Francisco: Harper San Francisco, 1991), esp. chaps. 2, 6-7, for other discussions of the quest for meaning through religious education.

2. J. Stanley Glen, *The Recovery of the Teaching Ministry* (Philadelphia: The Westminster Press, 1960), p. 29.

3. Ibid., p. 45.

4. Douglas John Hall, *Thinking the Faith: Christian Theology in a North American Context* (Minneapolis: Fortress Press, 1991), p. 13.

5. Stephen L. Carter, *The Culture of Disbelief: How American Law and Politics Trivialize Religious Devotion* (New York: Basic Books, 1993), p. 3; Bellah, et al., *Habits of the Heart*, pp. 220, 224.

6. Bellah, et al., *Habits of the Heart*, pp. 62-65.

7. This issue is discussed in a number of recent studies. See for example, Wade Clark Roof and William McKinney, *American Mainline Religion: Its Changing Shape and Future* (New Brunswick: Rutgers University Press, 1987), pp. 99, 170; Tex Sample, *U.S. Lifestyles and Mainline Churches: A Key to Reaching People in the 90's* (Louisville: Westminster/John Knox, 1990), pp. 28-29.

8. C. K. Ogden and I. A. Richards, *The Meaning of Meaning: A Study of the Influence of Language upon Thought and of the Science of Symbolism* (New York: Harcourt, Brace and World, 1946 [1923]), p. 47.

9. Robert Allen Warrior, "A Native American Perspective: Canaanites, Cowboys, and Indians," in R. S. Sugirtharajah, ed., *Voices from the Margin: Interpreting the Bible in the Third World* (Maryknoll, N.Y.: Orbis Books, 1991), p. 289.

10. Welch, "An Ethic of Solidarity and Difference," pp. 88, 90.

11. Sallie McFague, *Metaphorical Theology: Models of God in Religious Language* (Philadelphia: Fortress Press, 1982), pp. 4-5.

12. Chopp, *The Power to Speak*, pp. 111-12.

13. McFague, *Metaphorical Theology*, pp. 4-5.

14. Michael Polanyi and Harry Prosch, *Meaning* (Chicago: The University of Chicago Press, 1975), p. 66.

15. Margaret A. Farley, *Personal Commitments: Beginning, Keeping, Changing* (San Francisco: Harper & Row, Publishers, 1986), p. 14; Bellah, et al., *Habits of the Heart*, p. vii.

16. Hall, *Thinking the Faith*, p. 58.
17. Ibid., p. 63.
18. Ibid. For an extensive discussion of the relation of discipline and discipleship, see p. 65.
19. Brown, *Is Faith Obsolete?* pp. 42-63.

5. NURTURING HOPE

1. "Future looks bleak to anxious, pessimistic adolescents," *The Atlanta Journal/The Atlanta Constitution* (Thursday, January 14, 1992): B9 (Reprinted from the *Washington Post*).
2. Gordon D. Kaufman, *Theology for a Nuclear Age* (Philadelphia: The Westminster Press, 1985), pp. 4-11.
3. Ibid, p. ix.
4. Ilya Prigogine and Isabelle Stengers, *Order Out of Chaos: Man's New Dialogue with Nature* (New York: Bantam Books, 1984), p. 306.
5. The story of Community Church is drawn from an ethnography study I conducted as part of a project in congregational studies sponsored by Candler School of Theology, Emory University and funded by the Lilly Endowment.
6. Cf. The discussion of the role of teaching in the quest for meaning and vocation in Seymour, Crain, and Crockett, *Education Christians*, for another way to describe this process. They suggest that teaching involves actions of "discerning" candidly and openly the reality of our human situation, "considering" the adequacy of the meanings we have used to make sense of our situation, and "exploring" those experiences, images, stories, and concepts in our personal, cultural, and faith traditions for clues to meanings adequate to carry our hopes into the future. These steps lead teachers and learners through a process of "critical reflection" upon their situation, their tradition, and their dreams for the future; see pp. 150-53.
7. Jack L. Seymour, Robert T. O'Gorman, and Charles R. Foster, *The Church in the Education of the Public: Refocusing the Task of Religious Education* (Nashville: Abingdon Press, 1984), p. 137; Harris, *Fashion Me a People*, pp. 13-15.
8. Rollo May, *The Courage to Create* (New York: W.W. Norton, 1975), pp. 27ff.

A GUIDE TO REVISIONING LOCAL CHURCH EDUCATION

1. Lawrence A. Cremin, *American Education: The National Experience 1783-1876* (New York: Harper Colophon Books, 1980), p. 4.
2. RCIA is an adult education program of the Roman Catholic Church and Disciple is a Bible study program of The United Methodist Church.